C000147012

Poole in the
Great War

This book is dedicated to the memory of Dean Evans, the brother of Donna Harris. Taken from his family on 22 March 2016.

Poole in the
Great War

Stephen Wynn

PEN & SWORD
HISTORY
AN IMPRINT OF PEN & SWORD BOOKS LTD.
YORKSHIRE – PHILADELPHIA

First published in Great Britain in 2019 by
Pen & Sword Military
An imprint of
Pen & Sword Books Ltd
Yorkshire – Philadelphia

Copyright © Stephen Wynn, 2019

ISBN 978 1 47383 5 191

The right of Stephen Wynn to be identified as Author of this
work has been asserted by him in accordance with the Copyright,
Designs and Patents Act 1988.

A CIP catalogue record for this book is
available from the British Library.

All rights reserved. No part of this book may be reproduced or transmitted in
any form or by any means, electronic or mechanical including photocopying,
recording or by any information storage and retrieval system, without
permission from the Publisher in writing.

Printed and bound in England by TJ International, Padstow, Cornwall

Pen & Sword Books Limited incorporates the imprints of Atlas, Archaeology,
Aviation, Discovery, Family History, Fiction, History, Maritime, Military,
Military Classics, Politics, Select, Transport, True Crime, Air World,
Frontline Publishing, Leo Cooper, Remember When, Seaforth Publishing,
The Praetorian Press, Wharncliffe Local History, Wharncliffe Transport,
Wharncliffe True Crime and White Owl.

For a complete list of Pen & Sword titles please contact

PEN & SWORD BOOKS LIMITED
47 Church Street, Barnsley, South Yorkshire, S70 2AS, England
E-mail: enquiries@pen-and-sword.co.uk
Website: www.pen-and-sword.co.uk

Or
PEN AND SWORD BOOKS
1950 Lawrence Rd, Havertown, PA 19083, USA
E-mail: Uspen-and-sword@casematepublishers.com
Website: www.penandswordbooks.com

Contents

Introduction

Located on the south coast of England, Poole was never going to have too many prisoner-of-war camps for captured German soldiers in its midst throughout the years of the Great War, but it was still going to play its part in many different ways.

Some 10,000 men from the town answered the nationwide call to arms to protect their king and country, and around 1,000 of them never made it back to see their loved ones. This meant that hundreds of families across Poole lost fathers, brothers, husbands, sons, cousins, nephews and uncles; many of these individuals would have known each other with their families acquainted in some way, possibly socially or through work.

Everyone wanted to do their bit. Many of the town's men who couldn't or wouldn't enlist did something for the war effort through some kind of voluntary work. Many of these men enlisted in the Volunteer Training Corps, a kind of 'Dad's Army' unit. Many of the town's women took to working in the numerous hospitals as nurses, cooks, maids or cleaners, and so did some of the men, working as orderlies, stretcher-bearers or ambulance drivers.

To fight a war requires munitions of all shapes and sizes and, very quickly, factories started springing up all over the place to fulfil this enormous requirement, with most of the work being carried out by women as more and more men were needed to fight the war.

So many individuals, charities and well-meaning groups set up funds to raise money for the war effort. For example, there was the Poole War Distress Relief Fund, which was overseen by the local authorities, and even local schoolchildren helped raise money to purchase war certificates. Others, like the Poole

Sea Scouts and the 1st (Poole) Company, Dorset Volunteers, did their bit in a physical sense.

There was even the extraordinary case of a Poole woman who in 1916 appeared as a member of the Poole tribunal, the body that decided which men received certificates of exemption from wartime military service. By then she was already a member of the Poole Board of Guardians.

In many ways, the men and women of Poole were no different to those in thousands of other towns and villages that ran the length and breadth of the nation, although in some ways they were very different. However, when called upon to do their bit for their town and country, they did so in whatever way they could. By the time the war was over they had much to be proud of and, like those who had left Poole and gone off to war, they would remember those years and what they did for the rest of their lives. Many of them would have to do it all over again just over twenty years later, with memories of the Great War still fresh in their minds.

CHAPTER ONE

1914: Starting Out

The ancient borough of Poole was making preparations for the arrival of sick and wounded soldiers returning from Europe within just a week of the outbreak of war. Initial plans required eighty beds for use by the local Red Cross Society. Large homes where men could recuperate after having had their wounds treated in hospital were also needed, and the town's mayor, Mr G.C.A. Kentish, received many such offers.

On Saturday, 25 July 1914, the men of 'D' Company, 4th Battalion, Dorsetshire Regiment, otherwise known as the Poole

First Aid horse-drawn wagons.

Territorials, attended their summer camp at Bulford on Salisbury Plain. The battalion had a total strength of 764 officers and men. However, many of the units didn't get to complete that year's summer camp, having already been mobilized for war.

On Sunday, 26 July, with the outbreak of war just a matter of days away, the Poole Company of the Royal Garrison Artillery Territorials attended the divine service at St James's parish church. This was a customary practice on the Sunday prior to the men going off to summer camp. Some seventy-six officers and men from the Poole Company attended the service, including Captain W. Hatton Budge, Lieutenants F.W. Bee and P.C. Spain.

The men were due to begin their summer camp at Southsea Castle on Saturday, 1 August but this was cancelled on Thursday, 30 July when the Royal Garrison Artillery received orders to mobilize immediately and make their way to the headquarters

Men resting at camp.

of the Dorset Royal Garrison Artillery, which was situated at Weymouth.

On Friday, 7 August a recruitment meeting in Poole, which had been hastily arranged, was very well attended with an estimated crowd of some 500 retired soldiers, sailors and Territorials all keen to show their desire to do their bit, with a number of them re-enlisting. About fifty of the town's Militia Reserve left the following morning.

The town's mayor was quick to set up a War Distress Relief Fund, the committee of which would listen to any appropriate requests for emergency payments from the fund. The committee that would decide who got what included the mayor, the chairman of the Poole Board of Guardians, Alderman C. Curtis, Councillor F.S. Pridden from the Poole Guild of Help, the Reverend W. Willoughby from the Poole Free Church Council, Mr M.E.J. Pearce, the local Territorial Committee and Mrs Claude Lyon from the Women's Suffrage Societies, along with representatives from the Poole Trades and Labour Council, and the British Red Cross Society.

With the war in its early stages, excitement, exuberance and heightened awareness were all abundantly apparent. On Wednesday, 12 August, Karl Holm, a young German and an able seaman, was brought before the Poole magistrates charged with having failed to report himself to the authorities within the required time frame, as laid down under the Aliens Act 1914. The magistrates decided, after a brief consultation, that the young man should remain in the care of Police Superintendent Bowles while he in turn discussed the matter with the chief constable. Poole was one of the towns that had been designated as a restricted area, meaning that individuals from enemy nations were not permitted to reside there.

While the impact of the war had not yet had much effect upon the town, one man from Poole had just retired and was looking forward to a more tranquil pace of life. Timing, as the saying goes, is everything. Mr Mark Barnes of Poole had been a rural postman for a staggering forty-two years with his round stretching from the town all the way to Lytchett Matravers, but he had decided the time was right to hang up his postbag and enjoy his retirement and pension.

To mark the occasion of Mr Barnes' retirement, a number of residents to whom he had spent his entire working life delivering letters and other items of mail decided to make a presentation to him; this came in the form of an address, framed in oak, along with a purse of gold and best wishes for his long and happy retirement. The address reads as follows:

> To Mr Mark Barnes on his retirement from the position of postman after 42 years of service. We, the inhabitants of Lytchett Matravers, desire your acceptance of the accompanying purse of money in recognition of your long and faithful service as postman between this village and Poole, the duties of which you have carried out with unfailing fidelity and courtesy. We trust that you may be spared many years to enjoy your well-earned rest.

Mr Barnes had been born in the village of Lytchett Matravers, but lived with his wife Charlotte and their two children, Ethel and Reginald, at Lyndhurst, Garland Road, Longfleet, Poole. He did in fact have a long and happy retirement, twenty-eight years to be precise, before passing away on 19 November 1942, aged 89, at his home at 1 Longfleet Gardens, St Mary's Road, Poole. His son Reginald went on to become a Post Office clerk.

On the evening of Monday, 17 August, nineteen German merchant seamen were taken under military escort from Poole harbour to Dorchester. They were the crews of two German vessels that were impounded at Poole Harbour, the SS *Herbert Fischer* and the SS *Weser*. Poole was designated as a restricted area on the outbreak of war.

Poole quickly became a hive of activity, with local military units being mobilized as the war quickly became a reality. Captain D.C. Greenlees, the officer commanding the Poole Company of the National Reserves, requested that if anyone in the town had a service rifle, could they lend it to him to enable the men under his command to effectively practise their drill. Anyone willing to lend a rifle was asked to take it along in person to the Reserves Headquarters at the Artillery Drill Hall in South Road, Poole.

As if all that activity wasn't enough, some of Poole's yachtsmen had placed their own private yachts and motor boats, all of which were berthed in the town's harbour, at the service of the nation. This didn't mean that they were handing their treasured boats over to the authorities; just that their owners had signed up and joined the town's Volunteer Motor Boat Reserve.

It seemed that everybody wanted to do their bit; young or old, it didn't seem to matter. Even Bournemouth and Poole Sea Scouts got in on the act by carrying out evening patrol work between Sandbanks and Hurst Castle, although all Sea Scouts of school age who had been undertaking such duties were still expected to return to their classrooms when the schools re-opened after the summer holidays. Poole Secondary School re-opened as usual, but with the proviso that it would be handed over to the War Office for use as an emergency hospital if necessary.

Mrs Le Seuer, the Hon. Secretary of the Branksome Central Women's Liberal Association, set up a working party to arrange for the making of much-needed garments for sick and wounded soldiers and sailors who would be expected in the borough once casualties from Belgium and France began returning to the UK.

Even the National Union of Railwaymen got involved. The Poole branch of the union passed a resolution calling on the government to nationalize the nation's entire food supply, as well as coal and other essential commodities. Once this was done they wanted such goods sold at pre-war prices, and in the event of any shortages to serve out such items to all classes alike. Those at the meeting were also of the opinion that in the case of a national crisis, all classes should share the hardships and responsibilities equally. How that would work in principle was not discussed in detail.

It seems it wasn't just war that was the harbinger of death with men killing each other on the battlefields of Europe and beyond. Ordinary people were dying of a plethora of ailments, illnesses, disease and accidents throughout the United Kingdom, with Poole being no exception. The death of Mrs Sarah Elizabeth

Radcliffe, a 52-year-old widow who lived at 224a High Street, Longfleet, Poole, where she was a housekeeper to Mr Thomas Gallop, was proof of this.

An inquest into her death took place on the evening of Monday, 24 August in front of the Poole Borough Coroner, Mr E.J. Conway, at the Poole Poor Law Institution after she had been found dead in the hallway, laying in a position that suggested she might have actually fallen down the stairs. Mrs Radcliffe was identified by her sister, Mrs Annie Miller, who lived at Carter's Avenue in Hamworthy. She had last seen her sister on the Saturday evening before her death. Mrs Radcliffe had complained to her sister that the previous day she had been feeling a bit under the weather, suffering giddiness and diarrhoea. Mrs Miller also made mention of the fact that her sister's eyesight was not too good.

Mrs Julie Orman of 220 High Street, Longfleet, gave evidence that at about 6.30 pm on Sunday evening, her young daughter had told her that Mrs Radcliffe had asked for her, but she sent her daughter back to tell her that she was dressing and could not come. After delivering the message, she returned home and told her mother that Mrs Radcliffe wanted some brandy. Soon after this Mrs Orman saw Mrs Radcliffe looking out of her upstairs bedroom window; she shouted down that she was not feeling well and asked Mrs Orman to get her some brandy, throwing down a half-crown to pay for it. Mrs Orman, although not comfortable about having to enter a public house, agreed to do so in the circumstances. Mrs Radcliffe had asked her to knock on the downstairs back window on her return. With a small bottle of brandy purchased from a nearby inn, she returned to 224a High Street and sent her daughter to tap on the window as requested, but there was no reply and the window was shut. She also tried but once again, there was no reply. Mrs Orman assumed that Mrs Radcliffe, feeling better, had either gone to bed or had gone out for a walk to get some fresh air. About an hour later, she had seen Mr Gallop and a policeman enter Mrs Radcliffe's home.

Mr Thomas Gallop of 224 High Street, Longfleet told the inquest that Mrs Radcliffe had been his housekeeper for nine years, and that recently she had not been well, complaining of pains in her stomach. He advised her to get some brandy. On the Sunday evening he went out for a walk, and although she had not complained of feeling unwell, she asked him not to be long. On his return at just after 7.30, he found Mrs Radcliffe at the bottom of the stairs, dead. Her legs were pointing up the stairs and her head was resting on the floor of the hallway. From her position, it appeared to him that she had fallen down the stairs. He did not touch her, but instead went to inform the police. The court further heard from Mr Gallop that Mrs Radcliffe was a temperate individual, having, to his knowledge, some kind of alcohol maybe once every couple of weeks.

Dr W.T. Gardner arrived at the deceased's home at about 8.30 pm. He told the court that as far as he could tell, Mrs Radcliffe had been dead for about two hours, which would put her time of death at around 6.30 pm, about the time Mrs Orman had spoken with her. Dr Gardner explained that when he examined her, there was a wound on the side of her cheek and head in keeping with the impact of a fall. She had broken her neck. Death would have been almost instantaneous and was caused by a fracture of the cervical spine. Mrs Radcliffe was a large woman, which would have multiplied the force of the impact. He believed that she had fallen from the top of the stairs and had possibly struck the wall as she fell. The house was in darkness at the time and the steps were unequal and awkward, making the staircase dangerous. The jury concurred with Dr Gardner's summation, adding that the dangerous nature of the stairs should be brought to the attention of the borough municipal authority.

The day Mrs Radcliffe died coincided with the Battle of Mons; the first major British involvement in the war. By the end of that one day British casualties have been recorded as 1,600 killed and wounded.

The first man from Poole to be killed in the conflict was Private 6143 Sidney Charles Allen, who had first arrived in France on 16 August 1914. He was serving with the 1st Battalion, Dorsetshire Regiment when he was killed in action on 9 September 1914 and is buried at the British Cemetery in the village of Montreuil-aux-Lions in the Aisne region of France.

Dorsetshire Regiment cap badge.

Prior to enlisting in the army he had lived with his wife, Florence, who he married in August 1911 at Waterloo, Poole. The 1911 census showed Sidney working as a farm labourer and living with the Toop family at 23 Darby's Lane, Oakdale, near Poole.

The Toop family had two sons, Nathaniel and Walter. Nathaniel Toop attested on 14 February 1916 at Dorchester, three months shy of his thirtieth birthday, and the following day he was placed on the Army Reserve. He was mobilized on 29 March 1916 and posted as Private 17229 to the 7th Battalion, Dorsetshire Regiment the next day. He served in France with the British Expeditionary Force (BEF) between 20 July and

8 November 1916, and while in France was transferred as a Private (31817) to the 1st Battalion, Duke of Cornwall Light Infantry on 9 September 1916.

On 25 October 1916 Toop was tried by a Field General Court Martial for neglect to the prejudice of good order and military discipline. He was found guilty and sentenced to thirty days' Field Punishment No.1. A medical board held on 28 April 1917 found that he was no longer physically fit for war service, and on 19 May 1917 he was medically discharged from the army. His ailment is believed to have originated from 28 October 1916 near Béthune in France and resulted in him suffering pain in his back and legs, apparently as a result of exposure while on active service.

The youngest man from Poole to be killed during those first five months of the war was 19-year-old Private 9136 Percival Ernest Dyer. He had enlisted on 6 August 1914 and was serving with the 2nd Battalion, Scots Guards when he was killed in action during fighting between La Bassée and Armentières on Friday, 18 December 1914. He has no known grave, but is commemorated on the Ploegsteert Memorial in the Hainaut region of Belgium.

Prior to enlisting in the army, Percival had lived with his parents, James and Annie Dyer, at 44 Market Street. He was one of seven children, with four brothers and two sisters. The 1911 census showed Percival as a 15-year-old plumber's apprentice, and the family home was at 60 Garland Road, Longfleet, Poole. He went on to complete his apprenticeship and become a plumber and gas fitter for Mr Hardy of Poole.

Percival's brother Joseph had enlisted in the army on 4 September 1914 at Poole, and became a Gunner (11537) in the Royal Regiment of Artillery before being promoted to the rank of bombardier on 5 March 1915. His army service record includes a copy of a summons that was issued just ten days after his promotion at the Branksome Police Court due to an allegation that he was the father of a child born to Lilian Sealey on 1 November 1912. The court accepted that he was the child's father, and he was ordered to pay 2s 6d per week in maintenance towards the child's upbringing. These monies, as ordered by the court, were stopped from his army pay.

He served in France as part of the BEF between 26 July 1915 and 9 January 1918 and survived the war, being demobilized on 3 March 1920 and returning home to his wife at 44 Market Street.

On Saturday, 12 September there was a meeting of the Poole Territorial Association where it was decided to form a working guild that would make clothes for sailors and soldiers from the town of Poole. This would include men who were on active service, those who were still in training, and the wives and children who were dependent on them. There were a number of women on the committee, which included Lady Wimborne as president, Lady Lees, Lady Margaret Levett and the Lady Mayoress, Mrs Kentish.

There was a further meeting held on Wednesday, 23 September at the local office of the Territorial Association at 102 High Street, Poole. Lady Wimborne explained the importance of coordinating the work that was being carried out across the district by all women, so that it was known when and where the clothing they were making would be needed. To this end the cooperation with the Territorial Association was all-important, so that all the clothing made was directed to where it was needed most. She added that if their work was going to be effective and have any real worth, there could be no political or other divide between them, so they could wholly focus on the task in hand without any petty differences. The country was at war and if ever there was a time when everybody needed to pull together for the greater good, it was here and now. Lady Wimborne also expressed the considerable opinion among a number of the women that wartime stress wasn't just the preserve of soldiers, sailors and their families, and that due to the conflict, a number of people from across the town would experience stress; mostly the poor or those from the lower classes. Lady Wimborne had been informed by the Lady Mayoress that the National Union of Women Workers were working under the Mayor's Relief Committee, but her ladyship did not know whether they touched on the question of the provision of garments.

One thing that was agreed was the decision to name the new group the East Dorset Guild of Workers, and that the committee was to consist only of the presidents and vice-presidents. Mrs Trevanion was elected as the group's treasurer. A subcommittee consisting of Mrs Parish, Mrs Tatham and Mrs Kendall was appointed to cut out garments and to choose the materials, while Mrs Tulk and Mrs Trevanion were appointed to be those in charge of the receiving, storing and cataloguing of all donated clothing.

It was decided to consult with Mr Pearce of the Territorial Association to establish what clothing, comforts and necessities would be needed by the men of the town who were in military service. The decision concerning the distribution of garments among the poor of the town, other than the dependants of soldiers and sailors, was left to the Mayor's Relief Committee, and it was intimated that the distribution of leaflets and notices in the Poole area and rural districts would be undertaken by representatives of the two main political parties. It has to be remembered that all this work and coordination was carried out by members of the public and not at the bequest of or with assistance from any government departments.

An inquest took place on the evening of Friday, 16 October at the town's Guildhall before the Borough Coroner, Mr E.J. Conway, into the death of Mrs Ellen Foster, the wife of Harry Foster, a private who was serving with the Dorset Regiment. Before he had enlisted in the army, the couple lived as husband and wife at Strand Street, Poole and Harry had worked as a fish hawker.

Mrs Foster's death had occurred on the Thursday evening, and was both sudden and unexpected. Harry Foster, who had been posted to the Special Reserve, told the inquest that he had last seen his wife alive on the Wednesday evening, the day before she died, after which time he returned to barracks with his regiment. He had been granted leave of absence by his commanding officer on account of his wife's bad health as she had been unwell and complained of pains in her head. He said that she had a drop or two of beer, after which time she had been

Poole Town Hall.

sick. He had left 10s with Mrs Ruffell at Strand Street, Poole, in whose house she was staying, with instructions that if his wife was no better in the morning, she was to send for a doctor.

Private Foster explained to the court that he had brought his wife back from Portsmouth where she had been staying on the previous Monday evening. He also confirmed that a money order in respect of army separation allowance for the sum of £2 8s 6d was cashed by Mrs Ruffell and his wife the following morning.

Mrs Annie Ruffell gave evidence that on the Monday night Mrs Foster had complained of wheezing on her chest, but that she was quite sober. The following morning she took Mrs Foster to go and cash the money order. On the way back to her home, Mrs Foster called in at a pawnbroker's shop to redeem three pairs of earrings for which she had to pay 5s, but before going home the two women visited three public houses, Mrs Foster saying that she was cold and that 'a drop of something' might do her good. This was at a time when it wasn't usual for women to frequent such establishments, and certainly not on their own. They eventually arrived home at about 1.00 pm, but shortly afterwards Mrs Foster went out again, this time alone. The next time Mrs Ruffell saw her was at about 3.30 pm, when Mr Foster brought her home and it was clear to see that she was the worse for drink. He laid her down on the couch in the living room, which is where she remained until she was discovered dead the following day.

Dr W.T. Gardner Robinson was called to Mrs Ruffell's address where he examined Mrs Foster and found her to be cold and in a state of collapse, but before he could do anything for her, she died. He attributed her death to alcoholic poisoning, the same verdict that was then returned by the jury.

High Street, Poole.

The 1911 census shows a Harry and Ellen Foster living at Bowling Green Alley, Poole. There is no degree of certainty that this is the same couple as no record could be found on the Civil Registration Death Index for England and Wales covering the period between 1837 and 1915 for Ellen's death but, if it is the same couple, then they had four children: Alexander, Henry, Frederick and Samuel. The slightly contradictory yet intriguing aspect is that Harry is shown as being 55 years of age, but he earned his living as a fish hawker.

On Monday, 9 November a very interesting council meeting took place, including the town's mayoral election, and in part was due to points raised by Mayor Kentish. He began by commenting on the absence of two of their members, Alderman Lieutenant Colonel F.G. Wheatley and Councillor Colonel W.M. Sherston, the former being at Dorchester dealing with recruitment and the latter being on active service in charge of armoured motor vehicles. The mayor informed his colleagues that both men had left the decision as to whether they should be allowed to keep their places on the council or be replaced down to the current members. The mayor's view on the matter was that 'it would be very bad form to do so', a view that was echoed by all those present.

After being re-elected to the 'civil chair', the mayor said that the following year was going to be a difficult one and much harder than the current one. However, he trusted that as a council, they would, collectively and individually, do what needed to be done, even if some of their decisions would not be easy. Overall, it was simply a case of 'keeping their heads' and not panicking. There would be difficult times, but whatever was thrown at them they had to deal with in a calm and compassionate manner, and above all with courage. The ordinary man and woman in the street would be looking to them for leadership and direction, and they had to ensure that they did not allow a situation to arise where they became 'the captain of a rudderless ship'.

The mayor added that he had received a letter from the National Recruiting Committee, a body that had been formed to encourage recruiting throughout the country. So far, he

Poole recruitment Sergeant.

Recruits at camp.

said, the borough of Poole had done very well and that since 3 August 1914, not including reservists and those serving in Territorial units, a total of 653 had enlisted in the army and that currently around six or seven men a day were joining up. He said he didn't doubt that the comparatively low numbers of those now enlisting were down to the stories coming out in the press about the uncomfortable conditions in which men were being kept. This had now been recognized by the War Office and was starting to be addressed; a situation that he said he hoped would result in more men wanting to enlist.

The mayor then made a comment that was most definitely of the time, and although one that was met with agreement by his fellow councillors, wouldn't necessarily have been greeted in the same way today. He said

> we must remember that when we hear of those complaints from the camps and we see certain men coming to Poole and talking loudly about their complaints, it is probable that those are men who always grumble and will grumble

at anything. The men who first recruited were satisfied, or if not satisfied, they were prepared to clench their teeth and put up with it.

The time-honoured leadership quotation of 'Don't ask anything of your men that you would not first be prepared to do yourself' comes readily to mind.

The meeting also included a discussion concerning expenditure for the cost of hiring Special Constables to guard Poole waterworks, which was £15 a week, albeit that they were placed there on the advice of the chief constable of Dorset. The facility in question provided water for some 40,000 people in and around the Poole area. The mayor struggled to understand how some individuals believed that £15 a week was too much to pay for such a service. He added that if somehow their water supply was damaged or destroyed and 40,000 residents had no water, not only would they be unhappy and in danger, he doubted that too many council members would be able to forgive themselves for allowing such a situation to arise in the first place.

Poole Quay.

The meeting finished with the mayor having to scotch a rumour that someone they all might know had spread rumours that relief workers who had come into the Poole area were making 'a good thing out of it'. He said that on the contrary these individuals were working hard for the town and its people, and to suggest that they were doing anything less was 'absolutely wicked'. There were, he said, people from all walks of life and from all rungs of the social ladder who came to Poole to do their bit. Yes, they were paid, but they were paid for the hard work they did; nothing more nor less. Besides those of the town's civilian population who needed assistance, there were some 700 families of soldiers and sailors who also needed help that could only be properly facilitated by the use of such relief workers. To suggest that they were not doing in full what they were being paid to do was simply an outrageous slur.

December 1914 was the time when many had believed the war would be over. Done and dusted, victory assured, and all over with before Christmas. Who came up with that idea isn't known, but the fact that so many people actually believed it is the really worrying aspect. Not only was the war still going on, but so was normal, everyday life, yet the effects of the war, directly or indirectly, had started to become part of that as well.

On Tuesday, 1 December there was another meeting of the Poole Council. One of the topics up for discussion was again the issue of Special Constables guarding Poole's Municipal Waterworks. The discussion at the previous meeting had ended with the mayor throwing his full support behind the matter as he failed to understand how such an initiative could not be supported; the alternative was to him unthinkable. This time a different conclusion was reached.

The council was paying for twelve extra men who were engaged as Special Constables to guard the pumping station at Corfe Mullen and the various reservoirs around the borough. The cost, broken down, was 3s 8d per day per man, which was actually £15 8s, 8s more than had been claimed at the previous meeting. Up to that point the extra guards had been running for fifteen to sixteen weeks, meaning that the cost to the council

Sailor and family.

had been between £230 and £245. The Water Committee recommended that the present arrangement for policing the reservoirs and other similar waterworks throughout the borough be discontinued. Yet Councillor F. Hudson, the chairman of the Water Committee, said that he disagreed with the report's recommendations and hoped they would not be carried.

Alderman L.D. Ballard proposed an amendment that the guard be kept and it was seconded, but Councillor J. Waterman characterized the matter as an absolute waste of money. He pointed out that they had been assured that all the Germans in the country had been rounded up and that any damage done to any waterworks was not down to them. If they did discontinue the guard he did not think there would be a problem, but he added there was a possibility that certain gentlemen would try to create one. The use of the word 'gentlemen' suggested that maybe he was alluding to others present at the meeting.

Alderman Herbert Carter was certainly of the opinion that the guard be discontinued, unless it could be shown that there was some real and imminent threat to any of Poole's water facilities. The damage that had been caused, they were officially assured, was down to enemy aliens. One good assessment of the situation by Alderman Carter did come out of the discussion. His point was that even if there were some dangerous people in the area, if the council intended keeping a guard on these locations, they needed to rethink how they went about it. He clarified that he did not intend any slight to the Special Constables who he accepted were a group of hard-working and well-meaning individuals, but he felt that a skilled enemy agent would get the better of the men who were thus deployed.

Councillor W.P. Hunt agreed with Alderman Carter's opinion, stating that a man sitting in a house at night or walking round the boundaries was not a sufficiently effective way of guarding such premises. In the early days of the war it was a case of having to put in place some temporary measures to guard such premises, but they were always intended to be just that: temporary. They were never intended to be continued in the same format for the entirety of the war. He also pointed out that so far the cost of keeping such a guard had already run to over £200 and this was just one part of the waterworks, which meant the other parts were left neglected and that policy simply did not make sense.

Numerous other councillors had their say in the matter: some were for keeping the guard and others opposed it. Suggested amendments were voted on and other counter-amendments as the meeting veered from one aspect to another. At one stage the mayor, who was clearly in favour of keeping the guard, said that he protested against the speeches that had been made against the idea, that he disassociated himself from them emphatically, and went as far as declining to accept any responsibility if the guard was removed. Councillor R. Crab was quick to remind the mayor that the council was responsible as a whole, and he didn't feel that it was right for any one individual member to stand up and deny responsibility. Once all the talking was over, the proposed amendment to keep the guard was lost by a good majority and the Water Committee's recommendation was accepted and adopted, which meant an end to the Special Constables' guard duties.

CHAPTER TWO

1915: Deepening Conflict

Lance Corporal 392 A.J. Gambier of 'D' Company, 1st Battalion, Hertfordshire Regiment, part of the 4th Guards Brigade, wrote a letter to his brother, Mr E.E. Gambier of the King's Head Hotel, Poole which appeared in the *Bournemouth Guardian* on Saturday, 2 January 1915:

> I am still waiting further orders for another 'go'. We keep getting alarms, but I think we have them very well set now, and I don't think they will get any further this way. I expect you have seen by the papers the different accounts of our little affair, and I think it proves the old saying that one volunteer is worth forty pressed men. I am also pleased to hear your son Ted is doing his bit.
>
> If things were to happen in England the same as here, God help us. It's terrible, and, mark you, it would happen if it was not for a good many fools like me that have given their all to do the best they can. I have two mess mates with me, both Watford men; they have got six children each, and my eight makes twenty between the three of us, so God knows we have something to fight for, and I really think we can help them more by coming out than by stopping at home. I know I could not rest. Of course, you cannot expect that a man of your age and health could put up with the hardships we have here, as it affects the strongest, let alone anybody who has weak health, but I am pleased to hear you are doing, as every

man like you should do, what you can to encourage the recruiting of younger men. We can do with them, and, goodness, there are plenty still in England who ought to be made to come out.

A check of the 1911 census showed that Alfred James Gambier, who was 35 years old and a 'motor driver', lived at 219A High Street, Watford with his wife Ada and their eight children, whose ages ranged between 2 and 13.

Alfred had initially enlisted in the 2nd (Volunteer) Battalion, Bedfordshire Regiment on 8 March 1905, remaining with them until he joined the regular army on 16 April 1908 at Watford, and was first sent out to France on 5 November 1914, where he remained until 22 April 1915 before being sent back to England because he had been wounded. He was discharged on 15 April 1916 on termination of his engagement under King's Regulations 392 xxi. The following testimony was included on his army pension record:

> No.393 L/Corp. Alfred James Gambier is discharged on termination of engagement, and desires to take up his civil employment as a chauffeur. He is in every way a most trustworthy and conscientious man, with a very high sense of duty. He has gained the greatest respect from all his officers.

From the letter he sent to his brother, Alfred seemed very passionate about his soldiering and his belief that all able-bodied men should be made to go and fight. The fact that he left the army in April 1916, and not because of the wounds he had sustained a year earlier, suggests that he had tired somewhat of the senseless killing and mayhem that came with fighting a war. He also had a wife and eight children to think about, and having served in the army for eight years, he had definitely done his bit.

Mr Edward Evan Gambier, a servant in his younger years, was already 52 years old at the outbreak of the Great War. He was shown as being the licensed victualler of the King's Head

Hotel in Poole at the time of the 1911 census, an establishment he ran with his wife, Alice.

The annual meeting of the governors and subscribers of the Cornelia Hospital was held at the Guildhall, Poole on Wednesday, 24 February and presided over by the mayor, Councillor Mr G.C.A. Kentish.

Mr E.P. Belben, chairman of the committee, read out the report on the hospital for the year 1914, but before doing so commented on the fact that it was caring for men who were to be sent abroad to fight for king and country, but not only were they doing that, they were also treating the men sent back to England because they were either sick or wounded. This, he said, was something that the hospital should rightly be proud of.

Here is some of what the report contained:

> In estimating the work of the hospital for the past year, it is necessary to distinguish between civilian and military patients, and it will be gratifying for the subscribers to know that 331 civilian in-patients were treated during the year, an increase of 22 over the figures for 1913, and 82 more patients than the average for the past seven years.

The fact that the hospital was treating more patients compared with 1913 and collectively more than in the previous seven years doesn't necessarily portray a more efficient hospital. It could simply be that more people were living in the town, or that the advancements in medicine had increased the capacity of doctors' and surgeons' treatment:

> Twenty-three sick and wounded Belgian soldiers and 110 British soldiers have been received. The first party of British wounded were admitted on November 27th. In the month of September your committee received a most urgent appeal on behalf of sick and wounded Belgian soldiers, and at short notice, the outpatients' waiting room was furnished as a ward and accommodation added for ten patients. Beds were provided by friends, and

certain structural additions of a temporary nature were made to that part of the hospital. A contribution from the military authorities at the rate of 3s per occupied bed per day may be anticipated in respect of the treatment of the British soldiers, but as it appears probable to your committee that the actual cost could be 3s 6d per day, which has been the usual cost of in-patients, it is evident that additional funds will be urgently required for the treatment of soldiers as well as civilian patients.

On the afternoon of Tuesday, 16 February an impressive scene was witnessed by many people of Poole. The occasion was the burial of the second British soldier at Poole Cemetery. The Great War wasn't known in that way at the time; instead it was referred to as the European War and since its outbreak, two Belgian soldiers and one from Britain had previously been buried with full military honours at the cemetery.

Private 7120 Edward Sweeney of the 2nd Battalion, Royal Munster Fusiliers, was the first British soldier who had fought for his king and country, had been wounded in action on the battlefields of the Western Front and sent home to England to have his wounds treated, only to die in the town's Cornelia Hospital. On his arrival he had been mobile, even allowed to leave the hospital for periods of time to wander round the town, and in doing so he became acquainted with many local residents. Sadly, a relapse of his condition caused his death on Saturday, 13 February 1915.

Private Sweeney was 37 years old and an experienced soldier, sent out to France and Belgium on 23 August 1914, but to gain the full picture about him, one has to look back twenty-one years before the outbreak of the conflict, because it was in 1893 that he enlisted in the army and found himself serving as a private in the Royal Munster Fusiliers. He took part in the Second Boer War, 1899–1902, which he survived unscathed, even though he had been stationed at Ladysmith in Natal province throughout the entire siege (2 November 1899 to 28 February 1900).

The relief of Ladysmith, *1900: John Henry Frederick Bacon.*

When he returned to England after the end of the Boer War, he was placed on the Army Reserve and given a pension. As soon as the Great War began, he was called up, undertook some refresher training and was sent out to France and Belgium. He took part in the retreat from Mons, where the Royal Munster Fusiliers suffered some very heavy casualties. Between 23 and 30 August, ninety-eight of their men were killed in action and nearly double that number wounded. Soon after the retreat from Mons, he was transferred to the South Wales Borderers and later to the Connaught Rangers, the regiment he was serving with at La Bassée when he was wounded. He was in the trenches at the time, bent down to load his rifle, and when he stood up and raised his rifle above the parapet, he was shot by a German sniper, the bullet striking him on the right side of the forehead. Miraculously he wasn't killed, although he no doubt had a hell of a headache. Despite his injuries he walked for some 4 miles before climbing on board an ambulance cart. He hadn't travelled far when the cart was struck and damaged by pieces of an exploding German artillery shell. Still he didn't give up, walking for a further 2 miles before finally reaching a hospital where his head wound was treated and dressed and he was then sent home for further treatment. He arrived at the Cornelia Hospital on 27 November, where he died on Saturday, 13 February 1915.

For ten years before the war Sweeney had been a miner at the Fochriw No.2 Colliery at Merthyr Tydfil, close to where he lived with his wife and three children at Penydarren. On the morning of Tuesday, 16 February, as Private Sweeney was a Roman Catholic, a solemn Requiem Mass was sung by the choir at the church at Poole. There was a good turnout with a large congregation of mourners. The Reverend Father T. Hannigan not only took the mass but attended at Private Sweeney's graveside at the afternoon's ceremony, the deceased's body having been brought to the church the previous evening. The coffin-bearers were members of the ambulance section of the National Reserve.

Military funeral.

Starting from the church, the cortège slowly wound its way to the cemetery through Station Road and Longfleet Road. Marching slowly at the front was a firing party of thirteen soldiers from the Northumberland Fusiliers, who were stationed at Broadstone, under the command of Sergeant Bex. Behind them was the band, also from the Northumberland Fusiliers and under the leadership of Band Sergeant Davidson. En route they played the 'Dead March' from *Saul* at intervals; then followed the hearse containing Private Sweeney's coffin draped in a Union Jack, and then a carriage bearing his widow, her mother and sister.

It truly was an amazing turnout for a man who wasn't from Poole and, other than being in hospital and dying there, had no other connection with the town. It showed the people of Poole in their true light: caring, compassionate and considerate to a man who was only in the town because he had been wounded while doing his bit on the Western Front and ended up in the Cornelia Hospital. Flags were lowered to half-mast throughout the town,

Funeral leaving the church.

and children from the Longfleet School and the Roman Catholic school paid their respects by standing to attention and saluting the coffin as it passed by.

Also part of the cortège was Mrs Pratt, the commandant of the Red Cross Hospital, a wounded British officer and several wounded comrades of the deceased. There were a number of the South Wales Borderers who had worked alongside him on the Western Front and just happened to be home on leave at the time of the funeral. Sergeant Major Davies, who was in charge of the men present from the National Reserve, was in attendance, as was Lieutenant Marshall Hall. There were three nurses from the Cornelia Hospital, who were among those who helped treat the wounded soldiers. On arrival at the cemetery, the Roman Catholic burial service was read out, after which three volleys of shots were fired, followed by five buglers playing the *Last Post*, bringing a most impressive occasion to an end.

On the afternoon of Wednesday, 10 March a sheriff's meeting took place at the Church House, Parkstone for the purpose of forming a committee to obtain funds and to make arrangements to arm and equip the Poole unit of the Athletes' Volunteer Force. In opening the meeting, the sheriff stated that the establishment

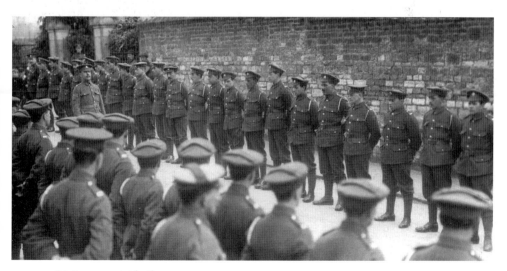

Lining up outside the cemetery.

of the corps was a form of local patriotism that deserved every encouragement. Mr Tilney Barton explained the corps' position, telling the meeting that it had received the official recognition of the War Office. They had a certain amount of flexibility to use their own initiative regarding the question of uniforms and equipment. The Poole unit had a strength of between 250 and 260, and had been formed at the insistence of Mr Neville G. Yeatmann.

The estimated cost of a uniform of tunic and breeches, along with a cap, was 29s, but each man would be asked to pay for his own breeches and puttees, while many men were more than happy to provide the entire uniform themselves. No man of military age would be accepted as a member of the corps unless he could provide a sufficient and lawful reason for not being able to undertake military service.

Major Reynolds provided the meeting with a brief outline of the work in which the corps would be engaged. The training involved drills, rifle-shooting, ambulance and basic first-aid, along with signalling classes. Others who spoke at the meeting included the Mayor Councillor G.C.A. Kentish, Councillor J. Mowlam, Lieutenant Colonel Lawrence, Colonel Lambert and the Reverend H.J. Graham. A committee was agreed upon, including the mayor, and they were asked to communicate with the War Office, calling their attention to the fact that the Poole unit of the Athletes' Volunteer Force was already doing government work, and asking for assistance with uniforms and equipment for the corps.

The mayoress of Poole, Mrs Margaret Kentish, wrote a letter to the *Bournemouth Guardian*, which appeared in the edition of Saturday, 17 April. The letter was an appeal to help fund a motor ambulance for the Red Cross in France:

Sir,

I have received a letter from the chairman of the Headquarters Committee of the Red Cross Society, and the Order of St John, asking if Poole borough will help

Motor ambulance.

to meet the urgent need for motor ambulances at the Front. The motor would be manned and run by the joint societies, and bear the name of the borough.

The price of a fully-equipped four-stretcher motor ambulance is £400. May I appeal through your paper to the citizens of Poole to help this much-needed and patriotic object. I shall gladly receive and acknowledge any sums, large or small; or subscriptions can be paid into the Poole Motor Ambulance Fund, at Lloyds Bank at Poole or Parkstone, by kind permission of the managers.

Yours faithfully

Margaret Kentish

Mayoress of Poole.

Undoubtedly such appeals always had more power behind them when an individual of some social standing in the local community was supporting and driving the initiative.

Red Cross Ambulance.

The *Bournemouth Guardian* of Saturday, 5 June reported that Joseph O'Neil and Tom Mason, both privates in the Duke of Wellington's Regiment, appeared before the Wimborne Police Court facing a charge of the theft of a case containing seven razors, a pair of opera glasses and a clock. The total value of these items was £4 and they all belonged to Mr A. Brown of West Street, Poole. The articles were stolen from a house known as The Firs during the absence of the owners, Mr and Mrs Brown, at Bournemouth on the previous Monday. Only two of the razors and the clock were recovered. A youth by the name of Ernest Holton, who was just 7 years of age and lived at King Street, Poole, gave evidence to the police of seeing a soldier who he now knew to be Private Mason put a razor on a wall as he was going home from Poole Park on the evening of 25 April.

William Ayer of Market Street, Poole said that while he was in the Potters' Arms, Hamworthy, Private Mason offered to sell him a razor for just 1s. Ayer said that he did not want it, but acting as he thought 'out of pure kindness' to a soldier, he sold it for him to a friend for 1s. George Kerslake, a shopkeeper from Poole, agreed to buy a clock from a soldier for 1s 3d.

Police Constable Reekes arrested both men at Poole: Private Mason at the railway station and Private O'Neil at the Anstey Arms. Neither man made any reply when charged with the theft of the razors, but the next morning Mason remarked: 'I don't know how they got in there; it would not have happened if we had not been drunk.'

Both men then changed their pleas from not guilty to guilty, with the mitigation that they were drunk at the time of committing the offence. Despite the prosecuting solicitor stating somewhat bizarrely that he did not wish to press charges against either of the two men and Police Sergeant Pride informing the court that the defendant O'Neil had recently been reduced from the rank of sergeant to that of private, the chairman of the bench found Mason and O'Neil guilty, calling them a disgrace to their uniform and sentencing them to fourteen days' hard labour.

Thursday, 15 July showed at first-hand how the effect of the war was gradually being brought home to communities up and down the country. It was for the people of Lower Parkstone as the community mourned the loss of Private Henry Homer James Hebditch-Carter, who was 31 years old, the son of Mrs Alice Carter of Highcliffe Mews, Britt Mews, Lower Parkstone. He died after a lengthy illness.

When he was just 17 years of age Henry enlisted in the 3rd Battalion, Dorset Regiment and saw active service in South Africa during the Second Boer War. When he returned to England, he was placed on the Army Reserve. At the outbreak of the Great War he enlisted in the army again, served with the Royal Army Medical Corps (RAMC) and was part of the BEF that was sent out to Belgium, where he took part in the retreat from Mons. While carrying a wounded soldier in the rear of his horse-drawn ambulance, a shell exploded nearby and literally blew his charge to pieces. Private Hebditch-Carter was thrown from the ambulance and left stunned and in shock. He lay on the battlefield for two or three days before being found by some of his colleagues, wet through and suffering on account of his prolonged exposure to the elements. In fact, he was in such a bad way that he did not recover consciousness until back in England and he woke up in bed having been taken to the Netley Hospital, near Southampton, Hampshire. After two weeks at Netley, he was taken to his home in Lower Parkstone where he stayed for a couple of weeks, but owing to his condition he was taken to a hospital in Bournemouth. After remaining there for a short period he returned home, but sadly there was no improvement and eleven weeks later he died. While at home he received a card from Queen Alexandra wishing him good luck, as well as a box of cigarettes and some tobacco. While in hospital during Christmas 1914, he received a festive card from Queen Mary, along with two nightshirts.

Netley Hospital.

Henry's stepfather, Mr Arthur John Carter, a carriage proprietor, was an army pensioner, having previously served with the 6th Dragoon Guards and been awarded three medals for his military service. Henry's only brother had also served in the military in the Munster Regiment, but he died in India in May 1912, some four years after having seen action on the North-West Frontier. When he died, the following paragraph was sent to his mother by his commanding officer and it also appeared in the Indian *Sunday Times*:

> The Munsters have had some unfortunate losses since the Regiment has been in Rangoon. This week one of the smartest soldiers in the barracks was carried to his resting place. He was Private H. Carter of 'H' Company, and was only 23 years of age. He was a splendidly-built young fellow, over 6 feet 2 inches in height and was the son of a well-known carriage-builder of Bournemouth. His company and battalion in general sincerely regret their loss, for Carter was very popular and was a daily example of what a British soldier should be.

The funeral of Private Hebditch-Carter was a well-attended affair. On leaving the church, the cortège wended its way to the Parkstone Cemetery and was headed by a firing party of fourteen from the Dorset Regiment, followed by the band of the 3rd Battalion, Dorset Regiment under Bandmaster W.V. Richards. Private Hebditch-Carter's coffin was next, draped in the Union Jack and carried by members of the Poole National Reserve under the command of Sergeant W. Hitching. The bearers were Corporal Marsh, Privates Gould, White, Rose, Foote, Robins and Holloway.

Besides members of his family, there was a noticeable turnout from the Poole Volunteer Training Corps and members of the National Reserve, and even a few wounded soldiers who were patients at the Cornelia Hospital as well.

On Saturday, 21 August the marriage took place at St Mary's Church, Longfleet of Percy Buckmaster, a private with the

Group of Soldiers.

2nd Battalion, Dorset Regiment and Lilian Mary Blandford, the only daughter of Mr H. Blandford, 174 High Street, Poole. The Reverend R.J. Large officiated at the service.

According to the 1911 census Percy was already serving with the 2nd Battalion, Dorset Regiment in India. By the time of his marriage, he had seen active service on the Western Front in France, where he had been wounded. He recovered fully from his wounds and was expected to return to France. The wedding was a splendid affair, with good weather making it a memorable occasion for all the right reasons, and was well attended by friends and family alike.

The British Army's Medal Rolls Index Cards covering the Great War show a Private 7607 Percy William Buckmaster who served with the 2nd Battalion, Dorset Regiment reaching the rank of corporal. While serving with the Dorsets, he also spent time attached to the Royal Munster Fusiliers and later transferred to the Machine-Gun Corps, where he was a Private (48692). He first arrived in France on 16 August 1914. He survived the war, was demobilized on 10 April 1919 and placed on Class Z of the Army Reserve, meaning men who were previously enlisted soldiers who had been discharged from the army.

On Saturday, 18 September a letter appeared in the *Bournemouth Guardian*, written by an unnamed member of the Poole Company of the Dorset Volunteer Corps:

'What use are the Volunteers?'

Sir,

In the volunteer orders for this week the need for more recruits is announced. May I be permitted, through your valuable columns, to make a very earnest appeal to all Poole men 'above military age', or those of military age who can show a genuine and approved reason for not joining any of His Majesty's Forces. In personally pressing these matters among some townsmen I have been met with the question of the heading. Let history answer with her record of the achievements of volunteers in our own and other nations. Be it also remembered that Volunteer Corps were the nucleus of our splendid Territorials. Is it too much to hope for a rekindling of that fire of patriotism that animated these men? Judging from the work given us to do for nearly twelve months past, it is evident that the naval and the military authorities here recognise the utility of the Poole Company of the Dorset Volunteers for their ability to render service to the state.

From the remarks of Colonel Harris at our inspection last week, coupled with those of Colonel Steward at the Malmesbury inspection, giving the War Office decision on volunteer inspections 'with a view to their employment in guarding waterworks, railways and certain prisoner' so as to release men of the Regular Army, it is obvious that a much greater sphere of usefulness is before all Volunteer regiments.

Our muster roll is at present lamentably small for an important port like Poole, and in view of increased work greater numbers are an absolute necessity for its due performance.

None who read Lloyd George's *Through Terror to Triumph* and the Press comments thereon can fail to realise the urgent need for all to do something in the tremendous crisis through which we are passing, the pressing necessity to concentrate on how to increase our own and our friends' efficiency, to refrain from all thoughtless chatter and trivialities, and to live, as we really are, under the shadow of a great danger.

I would entreat all available men to exercise some self-denial in these matters, to accept cheerfully the necessary preliminaries of squad drill, musketry inspection, etc, and come into our ranks and 'do their bit'.

Yours faithfully

A Poole Volunteer.

The name of the man who wrote this impassioned letter is unknown, but his pride and his desire for all available men from Poole to do what he saw as their duty is clear. No doubt its well-written prose encouraged a few men from Poole to enrol with the Volunteers and, as requested, 'do their bit'.

On Thursday, 23 September at the Poole Police Court, Levi George Cosh, the sub-postmaster at Canford Cliffs Post Office, was charged with having obstructed a number of naval officers in the lawful execution of their duties on Tuesday, 14 September, to which he pleaded not guilty.

Lieutenant Henry Burden of the Royal Naval Volunteer Reserve was the commanding officer of the guard ship in Poole Harbour. On the evening of 14 September he had been on sea patrol, relatively close to land, and for unspecified reasons he came in to shore and motored round the front at Canford Cliffs. While making his way along the Haven Road just before 8.00 pm, he noticed a parked mail van at the junction of Ravine and Haven Roads. The door of the sub-post office was open for the mail delivery, but because of the time a bright light from inside shone right across the road. Lieutenant Burden instructed Sub Lieutenant Friend to speak to the proprietor, advising him that there was too much light coming from his premises. Having done as instructed, Sub Lieutenant Friend told Lieutenant Burden of his conversation with the sub-postmaster.

As a result, Burden returned to the premises with his subordinate officer to find the door had been closed. He banged on it loudly, only to be told: 'The post office is closed, you cannot come in.' Burden repeatedly knocked on the door, but there was no response. While he was standing outside, the local postman knocked on the door and it was opened. Seizing their opportunity, Burden and Friend followed the postman inside. Burden located the sub-postmaster and asked why he had obstructed his colleague, with Mr Cosh simply repeating his earlier response. Burden pointed out that while he and his men were in the lawful execution of their duty, they were not bound by the same restrictions as members of the public and were entitled to enter any premises where a lighting offence was being committed. As that was happening here, they were perfectly entitled to enter and did not need his permission.

Burden told Mr Cosh he was surprised that he, as an employee of the Crown, would even consider obstructing an officer who was simply attempting to do his duty. Mr Cosh replied that he was not an officer of the Crown. Despite this reply, Burden said he had obstructed his officer, and he therefore asked him to accompany him to Poole so he could report the matter to the commander in charge. Mr Cosh refused, so Burden advised him that he would leave him no option but to arrest him.

Mr Cosh asked if he might have his supper first, but Burden refused and told him to put his coat on. He then went outside and waited in the hope that Mr Cosh would come along of his own free will, thereby avoiding being arrested. A short while later he joined Burden outside who was waiting in his car. They then drove to the officer in charge of the naval base in Poole, where on arrival Burden made his report. Mr Cosh was informed that he would have to return in a few days to answer the charge against him.

Mr W.H. Curtis, defending Mr Cosh, in cross-examination of Burden told the court that the obstruction consisted of his client refusing admittance and the subsequent conversation inside the shop. Mr Curtis maintained that at no time was the defendant told that he needed to put out his lights, neither did Burden say anything about being a naval officer while banging on the door. When he first entered with Friend, he made no mention of carrying out an arrest. Instead he spoke authoritatively because he had the authority of a naval officer, but Mr Cosh made no complaint regarding the manner in which he was addressed. It was simply a question of whether he would go with Burden voluntarily or under arrest. Mr Curtis's argument was that any possible obstruction took place for no longer than about fifteen minutes, and he conceded that Burden had driven Mr Cosh back home after the matter had been dealt with in Poole, as promised.

Friend told the court that he had been instructed by Burden to visit the Canford Cliffs Post Office and advise the occupant about the brightness of his lights. The premises were open, so he entered and came across some women. When he advised them of the problem with the lights they referred him to Mr Cosh, who was outside. As he began to go outside to speak with him, Mr Cosh came in and Friend drew his attention to the problem with his lights, to which Mr Cosh replied 'Get off my doorstep, the office is closed', at the same time trying to push him out using the door. Friend turned round and said: 'Don't do that, Mr Cosh.'

The mayor asked Friend 'Were you in uniform at the time?', to which he replied that he was. He continued that Mr Cosh persisted in pushing him out until the door was shut. He said he did not attempt to push the door open or shove it with his shoulder; instead he returned to Burden and explained what had transpired. They both returned to the Post Office and when they managed to get into the premises Mr Cosh said he thought they were volunteers.

Mr Curtis then conducted his cross-examination of Friend, pointing out that the light was showing because the door had been open but once it was closed, any light was minimal. He stated that Mr Cosh had taken steps to ensure all his windows were properly obscured during the hours of darkness. Mr Curtis then made the somewhat ludicrous statement that Friend did not introduce himself until he entered the shop for a second time, although it would have been abundantly clear to most that he was wearing a naval uniform. He further added that Friend just assumed his uniform would be sufficient to show that he was a naval officer. That is, of course, exactly what he had thought, and he had no reason not to unless Mr Cosh believed that Friend was impersonating a naval officer.

Despite Mr Curtis's comments and observations, at times appearing to contradict his own arguments, he initially seemed more contrite in his closing speech. He said that this was a most regrettable incident and he was instructed by his client to say how deeply he regretted anything he had done that could be construed as obstructing Burden or Friend from carrying out their lawful duty. Sadly, that's where the contrition ended and the comic theatre reappeared. He tried to suggest that despite Friend being in full naval uniform, including his peaked cap, Mr Cosh had no idea he was a naval officer, but assumed he was a member of the public. The comedy continued when Mr Curtis said that at no time did either Burden or Friend introduce themselves or explain who they were. Despite both men being in their naval uniforms at the time, he further added that Mr Cosh had believed Friend was nothing more than a chauffeur, but no observation was made regarding Burden being in exactly the same uniform.

Mr Curtis suggested there was no pushing by his client or any intention to obstruct, and insisting the door of the Post Office should be closed was acting in defence of government property in ensuring no-one entered the premises after closing. He desired to render every assistance in his power to any persons with authority, but when Burden spoke to him in a tone of authority in keeping with his position as a naval officer, as Mr Cosh was unaware of his status he probably resented being spoken to in such a manner and he hoped the bench would recognize this. Mr Curtis asked the bench to find that there was no deliberate and wilful intention on his part to obstruct Burden and Friend.

Last to give evidence was Mr Cosh, who began by saying that he had taken every precaution to have the lights in his place carefully screened and in doing so had incurred considerable expense. This was despite the fact that the downstairs of his premises was a Post Office, meaning that the cost of any such 'screening' was not his responsibility but that of the Post Office.

After hearing all the evidence, the mayor announced that the bench felt there was a certain amount of obstruction, but it was not considered to have been of a serious nature. A fine of 5s was imposed on Mr Cosh.

On Saturday, 2 October the sad news was received of the death of Private 1568 Harry Love Balston, killed in action while serving with the 13th Battalion, Australian Infantry, Australian Imperial Force, during fighting in the Gallipoli campaign. He had emigrated to Australia c.1890, and at the time of his death – Monday, 9 August – he was aged 41. Harry was buried at the 7th Field Ambulance Cemetery in Turkey. He served under the name of Harry Love.

His father, Alfred Balston, had been the mayor of Poole between 1876 and 1877, and was the owner of the Poole Twine Company. Harry also had three married sisters – Mrs William, Mrs Owen and Mrs Carter – who lived in Poole. He was also married and his wife, Irene Balston, lived in Wellington, New Zealand.

Saturday, 27 November saw a football match take place at the Breakheart Lane ground when the munitions workers of Longfleet St Mary's took on a team from the 12th Battalion, Worcester Regiment. Both had turned out strong teams, with Longfleet fielding Donald Slade, a well-known local footballer. In the early stages of the match, the men of the 12th Worcesters looked to be the better side and odds-on favourites to win. Their constant attacks pegged back the munitions workers, and it would surely be only a matter of time before the first of many goals was scored by the soldiers.

The Longfleet players gradually played their way into the game, making it a more balanced affair. Their play became more aggressive or, in today's football jargon, they 'pressed higher up the pitch' and were playing on 'the front foot'. Against the early

Munitions workers, ready for football.

state of play, the soldiers conceded two quick goals, scored by Norris and the star of the show, Donald Slade.

The second half went much the way of the first with the 12th Worcesters quickly back into their stride and gaining the upper hand, but unable to turn this into goals. Hutton struck a peach of a goal to put the home team into a commanding 3-0 lead, and despite the soldiers' best efforts, they could not respond in kind and the match ended with the munitions workers winning by a score of 3-0.

On Saturday, 27 November, 105 men from the Poole Soldiers Home were provided with afternoon tea and in the evening they were treated to an impromptu concert, the original programme being cancelled as a number of musicians failed to appear. Fifty men later enjoyed the sleeping accommodation provided, along with an excellent breakfast the following morning, after which a number of them attended mass at the Skinner Street Congregational Church. The Reverend F. Chalmers-Rogers, who took the service, asked various members of the congregation to invite some of the men to dinner, as had been done on previous

Munitions workers.

occasions. On the Sunday afternoon 170 men were entertained to tea at the Skinner Street Congregational Schoolroom, and in the evening the usual 'soldiers' social' was held at the Poole Soldiers Home.

Such events were long before the days of DJs or karaoke, and so the music provided was by way of musical instruments such as the piano or the cello, or short recitals with such well-known contributions as *Mate O' Mine* and *Goodbye Jim, Take Care of Yourself*, the latter having gone down very well some months earlier with men of the 17th Division who had been stationed in the neighbourhood. The line itself became an everyday greeting among them when they were deployed to the trenches of the Western Front. After light refreshments during the interval, which were enjoyed by about 100 soldiers, the evening's entertainment ended with an impassioned rendition of the National Anthem.

On the afternoon of Monday, 29 November an inquiry took place at the Guildhall in Poole before the Borough Coroner,

Mr E.J. Conway, into the circumstances leading to the death of 9-month-old Mary Elizabeth Bugden, the daughter of John Thomas and Rose Louise Bugden of Bell Lane, Poole. John Bugden was a serving soldier with the 3rd Battalion, Dorset Regiment.

The first to give evidence was Mrs Rose Bugden, who identified the body of the deceased as that of her daughter, Mary Elizabeth Bugden. She told the inquiry that at 9.45 pm on Saturday, 20 November, she slept in-between her 9-month-old daughter and another of her children who was 2 years old. The child, to the best of her knowledge, was in perfect health but when she woke up at about 7.00 am on Sunday, she discovered that her daughter was dead and lying on her right arm, facing away from her.

Doctor Malcolm Lamb from Poole told the court that he attended at the Bugdens' home on the Sunday just after 8.00 am at the bequest of Mrs Bugden, and found the child dead on his arrival. He estimated that the little girl had been dead for at least two hours, and her body was already becoming cold. He examined the child's body and found her to be well-nourished and there were no marks or bruises that he could see on her body. Mrs Bugden informed him that her daughter had never been ill, and was quite well when she put her to bed on Saturday evening. It was Doctor Lamb's professional opinion that the child had died from suffocation. When questioned by a member of the jury, Doctor Lamb explained that it was not necessary for the face to be discoloured in a case of suffocation.

During his summing-up, the coroner Mr Conway said that it was not advisable for parents to sleep with young children, especially babies, in their arms. Sleeping in such a manner led to the danger of a parent unintentionally suffocating their child, and although he understood the argument that sleeping in this way was warmer for the child than being in a cot during the cold, harsh winter months, it was still not advisable because of the danger of suffocation. The jury returned a verdict of death from suffocation, accidentally caused while in bed with the mother.

The 1911 census showed a John Thomas and Rose Louise Bugden living at 4 Pile Court, Poole with their 8-month-old son Alfred. John made his living as a fish hawker. A man from Poole with the same name and of the same age was found guilty of a number of thefts on 5 June 1899 at Wareham Magistrates Court before Mr Justice Phillimore and was sentenced to four calendar months' imprisonment, three of which were with hard labour.

On Wednesday, 8 December a successful and enjoyable smoking concert evening took place at the Heekford Park Drill Hall; not a way in which such an event would be described today due to the ban on smoking inside public buildings. The evening was in aid of the Poole Company of the Dorset Volunteer Regiment and included a full musical programme and refreshments.

Tuesday, 7 December saw the death of well-known local man Mr John Lane, who was 65 years of age and lived in North Road, Parkstone, having previously lived at 'Cullisse', Parkstone Road, Poole and who had for many years been associated with the firm of Carter & Co. Limited, who were involved in the manufacture of pottery ware, as their representative for the county of Dorset. He had also been the chairman of the Bournemouth and District Commercial Travellers' Association, was heavily connected to Longfleet Church and was a member of the Church Council and Building Committee.

Mr Lane's wife, Joanna, had died in August 1913, and their only son Hector Alan Lane, who was 25 years of age and a lieutenant in the 1st Battalion, East Lancashire Regiment, was killed in action on Thursday, 13 May 1915. The battalion spent the entire war involved in fighting on the Western Front, having first arrived in France in August 1914. He has no known grave, but his name is commemorated on the Menin Gate Memorial in the West-Vlaanderen region of Belgium. Before the war he had been a solicitor working in the tranquil surroundings of Singapore, but despite his good prospects in the legal field he returned home to England, joined the colours and received a commission with the East Lancashire Regiment. On Sunday, 19 September 1915, a beautiful stained-glass memorial window

Poole Volunteer Regiment marching.

provided by Mr John Lane was dedicated at St Mary's Church in Longfleet.

As 1915 drew to a close, nobody had the slightest idea what the next year would bring. Would it be the end of the war, the bloodshed and the killing? All they could do was hope.

CHAPTER THREE

1916: The Realization

The year 1916 was a notable one of the war. It saw the implementation of the Military Services Act, the Battle of the Somme, Germany attempting to make peace, and 187,735 of the nation's men being killed, which equates to 514 each and every day of the year.

The Military Services Act 1916, which had been put forward by the then Prime Minister Mr H.H. Asquith in January 1916, came into being on 2 March 1916, and meant that for the first time in Britain men could be conscripted into the army to undertake military service. Prior to this all military service had been of a voluntary nature, but in a time of war a nation needed an army to sustain itself against a determined and dogged enemy.

The Act specified that all men who were aged between 18 and 41 were liable to be called up, but as with most rules there were also exceptions. This didn't include married men, widowers with children, those serving in the Royal Navy, a minister of religion or a man who was working in any of the numerous occupations that had been designated as reserved. Only two months after the Act came into being, a second Act determined that married men were liable for military service, and a third Act in 1918 increased the age limit to 51.

If a man or his employer had an objection to him being called up, they could apply to a local military service tribunal for an exemption. If such an application was rejected in whole or in part, there was a right of appeal to a county tribunal.

Military Services Act 1916 poster.

A man could make such an appeal on specific grounds: that he was already undertaking work of national importance; that his business would suffer unduly if he had to enlist; domestic hardship; that he was medically unfit to undergo such service; or because he had a conscientious objection, which was usually connected to religious beliefs. Ironically, even though it was a prescribed reason to appeal against having to undertake military service, it was rarely allowed.

In almost four months between 2 March and the end of June 1916, a staggering 748,587 men applied to tribunals for exemptions from having to undertake military service. In the same period of time, a similar number of men enlisted in the British army.

On the afternoon of Monday, 24 January a meeting took place at the Poor Law Institution of the Poole Rural District Council. As was usual with such meetings, there were many different topics on the agenda, including Payment for Extra Services, State of the Roads and Widening of the Roadways, to name but a few. One item on the agenda particularly caught the author's eye. It was under the heading 'School Boys and Farming'. A letter had been received by the Poole Rural District Council from the Shaftesbury Rural District Council with the following resolution passed by them and and asking the members of Poole Council to approve the same:

> That the Dorset County Council be urged to at once take steps as may be necessary to secure the release from school of any boy of eleven years of age and upwards, on the Local School Attendance Committee or School Managers being satisfied that such lad is to be regularly and profitably employed.

One council member, Mr Clark, commented that he believed boys were being kept in school too long when they could be better employed doing useful work on local farms, especially in wartime Britain when labour was needed for agriculture, which in turn provided vital foodstuffs for the nation as a whole. Mr Clark said that he had 'much pleasure' in proposing that the council adopted the motion. However, as with all such contentious matters, not everyone on the committee was in agreement, as might well be expected.

Mr Bollam, for one, was against it. He felt that 11 years of age was far too young for a boy to be leaving school and his education behind him, but Mr Clark's motion was seconded by the Reverend Sharp and the chairman was in support of it as well. He was of a mind that for boys to become good workers they needed to start work before they were 14 years of age, which was a trait and an ethic that was of great benefit to the younger generation, not only when they were starting their employment, but later in their life when they themselves were parents.

Mr Curtis said that he was prepared to support the motion up to a certain point, but he believed the age mentioned was too young. He was not an advocate of boys leaving school at 11, but they were in the midst of difficult times. The country needed to look to the future and realize the importance of education for its youngsters, who then had more chance of doing great things for their country, economically as well as commercially. He added that Germany had certainly recognized the importance of education for her own youngsters. After the war was over, there would be another war, one for commercial superiority, and if they economized too much in education now, he felt they ran the risk of being left behind in a commercial sense as well. He disagreed with the motion unless the age was raised to 12.

Boys making barbed wire.

Mr Sharland agreed with Mr Curtis, and said that there were hundreds of boys who should be kept in school and hundreds more who should not. There were some boys who would undoubtedly not benefit from staying on any longer in school than they legally had to. What he referred to as 'those dull boys', he felt would be better employed spending their time working as farm labourers. The question was asked, maybe a tad tongue-in-cheek, how one would differentiate between a boy who was dull and one who wasn't. Mr Sharland didn't elaborate any further. Mr Bollam seconded Mr Curtis's suggested amendment, Mr Clark withdrew his motion, and the amendment was carried.

On the afternoon of Tuesday, 15 February, the monthly meeting of the Poole Harbour Board of Commissioners was held at the harbour offices, with the Mayor, Councillor G.C.A. Kentish presiding. As usual, numerous different but relevant points were discussed. One of the headings on the agenda was government and harbour dues.

There appears to have been some kind of discourse between the Poole Harbour Commissioners and the Bristol Channel Dock Owners' Association concerning the issue of payment of harbour dues. The president of the former wrote a letter to the Dock Owners' Association referring to a matter in which they had agreed to receive a report from them. The letter concerned the government being exempt from having to pay any harbour dues. The Bristol Channel Dock Owners' Association had decided they were going to send a deputation to the commissioners to discuss the matter.

The mayor said that at their previous meeting the board had decided not to send a representative, but instead wrote to the association expressing their pleasure at receiving any intimation as to the progress of the deputation. Mr Belben did not think that it would be worth sending a representative as it would have no effect. Mr E.E. Kendall said that if he remembered rightly, Mr Stiff had offered to go at his own expense, which he felt was a good idea. There were different views around the table: some of the members were for sending a representative to a meeting of the Bristol Channel Dock Owners' Association, while others weren't. Ultimately the decision was taken not to send anybody.

In some respects it seemed a pointless discussion: all that talk about something that hadn't actually happened, as in the Bristol Channel Dock Owners' Association not sending the Poole Harbour Board of Commissioners a report that they said they would on a subject in which ultimately they had no say. If the government was exempt from having to pay any harbour dues, that was a matter between them and the Board of Commissioners of Poole Harbour.

Poole Harbour had, in previous years, been the main British trading port, certainly along the south coast, and at the beginning of the nineteenth century, it had been the town's singular most important employer. However, the harbour had regained some level of importance during the Great War through its use by the Royal Navy.

On the evening of Thursday, 9 March there were seventeen applications heard before the Poole Borough Military Service Tribunal, which was chaired by the mayor, nine other members who were either councillors or aldermen, together with a military representative who in this case was Lieutenant A.S. Marshall Hall.

Of these cases, a number of them were heard in private; a possible indication that the individuals concerned were prominent local figures, or that they were embarrassed at making such an application and didn't want anybody to know. Out of the other cases, two were told they would have to join the non-combatant corps, usually an indication that the men concerned were conscientious objectors. Two men were already working in certified occupations so they didn't have to enlist, although that was liable to review if they changed jobs. Two men received one month's exemption, two more received three months' exemption, another was adjourned, one was withdrawn, and one man was given a total exemption on medical grounds.

In the subsequent reports of cases that were heard by the tribunals, the men in question were never named. In fact after the war, the government instructed all local authorities to destroy any and all records they had in relation to military tribunal cases. Why is one of those $64,000-dollar questions. Here is an example of one of the cases heard by the Poole military tribunal.

Sometimes it didn't appear that everybody was being treated in the same way. An appeal was made by the local authorities in Poole for a clerk who worked in the town clerk's office who was engaged in accountancy work and educational administration. The reason put forward in support of the man in question was that he could only be replaced by a person who had considerable training in his areas of expertise. Personal but unspecified domestic grounds were also proffered as a reason to keep him from having to undertake military service.

The town clerk pointed out that the man was passed for home service, which meant that he could remain in civil employment and receive two months' notice. On the suggestion of the town clerk, the man went to Dorchester and was passed for general service. That being the case, the town clerk asked the tribunal to treat him as if he was for home defence. The man was granted two months' exemption.

Dorchester Camp.

Poole Council had authorized the town clerk to make representation in support of claims relative to persons engaged in the teaching profession. With regard to one of the headmasters, a single man, the reason assigned for asking for an absolute exemption was that the work performed by headmasters of public elementary schools was essential in the national interest, and it was necessary in the interests of education that the services of this headmaster should be retained in the school. The town clerk pointed out that at the outbreak of the war there were thirty-nine teachers of military age. Sixteen had enlisted and a further seventeen had attested. Of the latter number, four were head teachers, nine were certified assistant head teachers, and four were uncertified assistant head teachers. The tribunal, having given the facts due consideration, allowed two months' exemption.

Poole Council also put forward a claim for absolute exemption for, of all people, a water rate collector, arguing that his work was important and necessary, and further that the place of the man in question could only be filled by a person with considerable previous training in the same field. Somewhat astonishingly, not only did the tribunal not kick out the application, they provided the man in question with two months' exemption. Even looking at this almost 100 years after the event, it is somewhat difficult to grasp the concept that a man going from door to door, collecting money for water rates, would have required such in-depth training that they were nigh on impossible to replace! After all, how much training could one man need to knock on a door, ask for some money, go back to his office and fill out the relevant paperwork?

A 30-year-old man from Upper Parkstone made an application for absolute and complete exemption. He addressed the tribunal members with the following words:

> My application is for absolute and complete exemption. My conscientious objection to taking part in the war, either directly or in a non-combatant capacity, is my belief in the sanctity of human life. I feel so strongly that whatever the decision of the tribunal may be, and fully

realizing the consequences that may follow my decision,
I solemnly and sincerely state that I should prefer any
penalty that may be inflicted rather than place my mind
and my conscience under military orders.

The man, when asked by the mayor, replied that he did not belong
to any particular religion. More questions followed before the
mayor informed him that he would be exempt from combatant
service, but not non-combatant service. The man intimated that
he would appeal the decision.

Another man from Upper Parkstone, who by way of
occupation was a painter, also applied for an absolute exemption,
stating that he could not conscientiously undertake combatant
or non-combatant service, nor could he assent to his normal
occupation being made a condition of exemption as this would
convert his work into an acknowledged contribution to the
organization of a nation when prosecuting war. In reply to
questions, the applicant said he did not belong to any religious
body and objected on moral grounds, and that he had held these
beliefs for some time. The mayor asked the man whether he had
served in the Territorials, to which the man replied that he had.
'Did not your conscience tell you then?' the mayor enquired.
'I was a kiddie at the time and did not know what I joined for.'
'How long were you in the Territorials?' 'Five years,' the man
replied. He was exempt from combatant service only.

On the evening of Thursday, 27 April, the day that 623
British servicemen died during the Great War, there was another
fatality that hit home even more painfully because it involved a
young boy from Poole. Jesse Barfoot of Market Street, Poole
was playing with two of his friends near the railway line that ran
between Parkstone and Poole when he strayed onto the track,
was hit by a train and decapitated, his head being separated
from his body. One of the other boys, William Craven, was more
fortunate, the train missing him by a fraction.

The death of Jesse Barfoot was the subject of an inquiry at the
Poole Guildhall on the following Saturday afternoon, and was
heard by the borough's coroner, Mr E.J. Conway. Mrs Barfoot,

Jesse's mother, confirmed that he was 9 years old and she had last seen him on the afternoon of the day he died, when he had been in his usual state of health. She added that he was a boy who never usually travelled too far away from his home, and to her knowledge he never went onto or near the railway line.

William Craven, who was 12 years of age and lived at 61 Market Street, Poole, told the inquiry that on Thursday afternoon he and a little boy named Spiller went out with Jesse to the Ladies Walking Field at about 4.00 pm. They climbed over the fence onto the banks near the railway lines. They were gathering fir cones and picking up sticks when Jesse went onto the line near 'The Bunny' to get a piece of wood. They then played about on the line and did not see the train coming, then crossed over the train track and were sitting on the bank, outside the actual train lines. William did not recall hearing a train whistle, but the little boy Spiller called out to him and Jesse Barfoot that the train was coming. William and Jesse were only about 2 yards apart at the time as Jesse was kneeling down and didn't appear to react. William repeated what Spiller had said about there being a train coming and Jesse replied 'What?', but by that time the train was already upon him. He stood up but didn't move off the railway lines and the train hit him.

Sidney Hayball, the driver of the train in question, told the inquiry that he was driving the 5.22 pm train Bournemouth West when he began his approach towards what is known among railwaymen as bridge No. 7. As he did so he saw three heads pop up above the level of the rail. He immediately blew the train's whistle and applied the brakes to bring the train to a safe standstill. He noticed that the boys appeared to be looking towards Poole, but as soon as he sounded his whistle they immediately turned their heads round towards his train. All three of the boys were down in a dip, which was even lower at the point of the bridge. As he passed he felt no impact. As the train came to a halt he sent its fireman back down the track to see if he could find the boys and to render any assistance he could.

Arthur Alfred Young, the train's guard at the time of the incident, told the inquiry that as soon as he heard the driver sound his whistle, he immediately applied the automatic brake and also applied his handbrake manually. On looking out of the window of the train, he saw two lads run across the line after the train had passed. When the train stopped the fireman approached him and told him that he believed that one of the boys had been hit as he had initially seen three of them. The fireman and the guard made their way back down the track towards bridge No. 7, which was where they found the body of a young boy, but there was no head as it had been completely severed. Neither the guard nor the fireman could find the boy's head anywhere, so they marked the spot of the body on the ground before picking it up, carrying it a short distance and placing it under a nearby tree. They then took the other two boys, Spiller and William Craven, back to Poole in the guard's van and reported the matter at the station.

Police Constable Smith gave evidence that at about 6.00 pm he went to Poole Park, which he was told was where Jesse Barfoot's body had been left, and found it partly covered with a small sack. He then found the mark left by the guard and the train's fireman to indicate where they had originally found the boy's body. Constable Smith conducted a search of the area and eventually found the missing head which was about 20 yards away from where Jesse's body had originally been found. He then removed both to the town's morgue.

In his summing-up the coroner said that he sympathized with the friends and relatives of the poor little boy, but he could not apportion any blame in any direction against any individual. It seemed to him to be nothing more than a tragic accident. The boys were on the line and they ought not to have been there, but of course boys would be boys. He hoped that this tragedy would serve as a warning to other boys not to go too near to the railway lines and the dangers that they posed. The jury returned a verdict of 'Accidentally killed by a passing train.' They also expressed the opinion that the driver was free from all blame and should be commended for the smartness with which he pulled up the train.

At the time of the 1911 census, Jesse Barfoot was 4 years of age and lived at 20 Stanley Road, Poole with his parents, William and Bessie Barfoot, his four brothers, William, Fred, Walter and Albert, and his two sisters Winnie and Nellie. Another brother, Arthur, was born on 13 January 1913. His father William was a labourer.

The author searched the British Army's Service Records covering the period of the Great War and discovered a William Barfoot who enlisted in the army on 17 August 1915 at Whitehall, London, and became a Private (292582) in the 705th Company, Labour Corps. He was 40 years of age and was living at 42 Market Street, Poole. This gives the correct age for Jesse's father, and the same street that Jesse was living in at the time of his death. On 18 October 1918 he was transferred to No. 5 Water-Boring Section of the Royal Engineers as a Pioneer (117444). He was finally demobbed from the army on 25 February 1919 at Chatham, and placed on the Army Reserve.

What a sad irony for a parent to have to deal with. A man goes off to fight in a war to help his nation remain free and stay out of the grip of a determined enemy who is hell-bent on defeating them. He survives and returns home to the bosom of his loving family, only to discover that one of the very people who he was fighting to keep safe, his own son, had been killed in a tragic accident.

Thursday, 25 May saw a number of men appear before the Poole borough tribunal, which was held at the town's Guildhall and presided over by the mayor of Poole with another member of the tribunal being a Mr Sharland.

One of the cases being heard that day was of a farm bailiff and sanitary contractor. It is not clear on what grounds the man was requesting a certificate of exemption, but he was granted the same for a period of five months until 1 October 1916. The man in question was the son of Mr Sharland, one of the men who was actually part of the Poole borough tribunal on that occasion. Mr Sharland did remove himself from the tribunal when his son's case came to be heard, although it is hard to understand what he was actually doing there in the first place. Having said that, it is hard to understand why the case was brought before the Poole borough tribunal at all. Surely with the family connection, there was always going to be a certain level of bias, whether that was conscious or subconscious. How being a farm bailiff as well as a sanitary contractor warranted a five-month exemption is mind-boggling. There were six men including Sharland who had their applications heard on the day, and out of the other five men only one of them received the same exemption that he did.

On Wednesday, 7 June a garden sale and gymkhana took place in the grounds of St Peter's House, Parkstone. Permission for the grounds being used in such a manner was given by Reverend the Hon. R.E. Alderley. The reason for the event was to raise money on behalf of the Parr Street Sewing Circle, which was part of the Dorset Guild of Workers. The monies raised helped them in their efforts to knit items for British soldiers from Poole who had been captured by the Germans and were being held as prisoners of war. The leader of the group, Miss Ada E. Briggs, who had been assisted by other members of the group, had organized a really enjoyable day for those who attended. The event was opened by the Lady Mayoress, Mrs Margaret Kentish, who was first introduced by Reverend Alderley. He spoke of how ready and willing she was in coming forward to open such events throughout the borough, especially ones that helped raise money for work relating to the wounded soldiers and sailors of Poole.

The mayoress was warmly greeted with a most cordial reception by those present, and it was clear that she was suitably impressed by the work done by the women of the Dorset Guild of Workers, especially as its headquarters were in Poole. She also spoke of the large number of parcels that the group was sending overseas, mainly to the men on the Western Front but further afield as well. She mentioned that there were some 400 men from Dorset being held as prisoners of war in Germany, and each one of them received a parcel every week from the Dorset Guild of Workers. This meant that all the ladies' hard work could not be carried out without fund-raising events such as this.

July 1916 saw numerous families from Poole receive news of their loved ones serving overseas. Mrs Mina Budge of 'Devana', Seldown Road, Poole, received news that her son, Captain

Herbert Lionel Budge of the Royal Scots, had been killed in action. One of his brothers, Captain William Hatton Budge of the Royal Garrison Artillery, was the magistrates' clerk for Poole. He had followed his father into the legal profession.

The Commonwealth War Graves Commission website records Herbert Lionel Budge as a lieutenant colonel who was 38 years of age and serving with the 12th Battalion, Royal Scots, when he was killed in action on Thursday, 13 July 1916 and was buried at the Carnoy Military Cemetery in the Somme region of France, suggesting that he was killed during the Battle of the Somme. He was also married, and his wife, Florence Louise Budge, lived at 'Penhale', Poole. He had also served during the South African campaign, better known as the Second Boer War. It somehow seems strange that Herbert's mother was informed of his death when he was a married man.

The war years had been harsh for Mina Budge, because not only had the war taken one of her sons, but her husband, Philip Edward Lionel Budge, who was a solicitor in the town, had died at the age of 65 on 16 April 1915.

Mrs Ellen Lake of 13 St John's Road, Heckford Park, Poole, received the sad news of the death of her son, Private (3/7905) Edwin Lake of the 1st Battalion, Dorset Regiment, who was killed in action on 10 July 1916 during the Battle of the Somme. He has no known grave, but is commemorated on the Thiepval Memorial in the Somme region of France. Mrs Lake had already lost one of her sons in the war. Fred Lake was a Lance Corporal (3/7750) in the 5th Battalion, Dorsetshire Regiment when he was killed in action at Gallipoli on 8 December 1915, and buried at Hill 10 Cemetery in Turkey.

The 1911 census showed that Ellen and her husband, John Lake, had a total of fifteen children, of whom twelve were still alive at that time but only four of them – Frank, William, Harry and Percy – were still living at home. Another of her sons, Bertie, served in the war as a Private (92/082) in the 154th Company, Labour Corps. He enlisted on 11 December 1915 and arrived at Le Havre, France on 5 October 1916. He returned home on 20 January 1919, and was demobbed on 1 February 1919 at

Fovant dispersal unit. By the time the war was over another of her sons, Charles Lake, a Lance Corporal (27813), 1st Battalion, Duke of Cornwall's Light Infantry, who had previously served as a Private (23180) in the Somerset Light Infantry, had been killed in action on 18 April 1917 on the Western Front in France. He has no known grave, but is commemorated on the Arras Memorial in the Pas-de-Calais region of France.

Mrs Brown of Longfleet Road, Poole received news that her husband, who was serving in the Dorset Regiment, had been killed in action. No sooner had the family taken in the enormity of that news than they received further reports that he was in fact alive and had only been wounded and was being sent home to England to have his wounds treated. Prior to enlisting in the army, he had worked as a tram conductor and an outside porter at Poole railway station. The confusion possibly arose because the Commonwealth War Graves Commission website shows that there was a Private (7643) Frank Brown who also served with the 1st Battalion, Dorsetshire Regiment. He was 41 years of age; a married man who before going off to war lived with his wife Annie Helena Brown of 'Kensington', Longfleet Road, Poole. He was killed on the first day of the Battle of the Somme, 1 July 1916.

In response to an appeal by the mayor of Poole, Councillor Kentish, many of the town's vehicles, including the tramcars, came to a halt for a couple of minutes at 12 noon on Friday, 4 August while shop-owners closed their premises for an hour to commemorate the second anniversary of the beginning of the Great War.

Services were held at various churches and chapels throughout the borough, with the mayor and other members of the corporation, which included the deputy mayor, Councillor J.A. Hawkes and other senior officials, attending a divine service at St James's Church, commencing at 12 noon. It was an impressive affair, with the singing of four well-known hymns including *O God, Our Help in Ages Past*. The Reverend H. Lawrence Phillips delivered an impressive and thought-provoking sermon, which in essence looked at the first two years of the war and was a precis of the main events. Clergy and ministers from other religious denominations also took part in the service.

The day's commemorations didn't end there. In the evening there was a united service held on the town's quay, with the choirs of St James's and St Paul's Church accompanied by other choirs of the nonconformist churches, who had first assembled at St James's Church before making their way, along with clergy and ministers, to the quay. The service was an impressive spectacle, with a crowd of some 1,500 in attendance.

The Battle of the Somme began on 1 July 1916 and by the time it had finished some five months later, on 18 November, Britain had sustained some 435,000 casualties. The battle was in fact made up of thirteen smaller battles that took place in three phases. The week before the battle began, the British bombarded the German defensive lines almost around the clock with the intention of obliterating their positions, along with killing as many Germans as possible. Once this had been achieved the plan was for the British troops to simply march across no man's land into the destroyed German trenches, although that is not what happened. The artillery bombardment proved so ineffective that Britain sustained somewhere in the region of 50,000 casualties on the very first day of the Battle, 20,000 of whom were killed. Four of these men were from Poole.

The youngest of these was 18-year-old Private 16103 Cecil Crane of the 1st Battalion, Dorsetshire Regiment, who was buried at the Serre Road Cemetery No.2 in the Somme region. His mother, Mrs Mary Ann Sophia Crane, lived at 3 Little Croft Road, Upper Parkside, Poole.

The 1st Battalion, Dorsetshire Regiment had first arrived in France, at Le Havre, on 16 August 1914 as part of the BEF. From there, they made their way into Belgium and were involved in the fighting at the Battle of Mons. Once the decision was made to retreat, the battalion was involved in the rearguard action that allowed so many of their colleagues to make good their escape. For them, there was to be no respite. They were on the move for sixteen consecutive days, during which time they covered a distance of some 220 miles. Despite their tiredness and the lack

A group of young soldiers.

of any proper meals during that time, on 4 September, having reached the town of Cagny in France, they finally managed to halt the German advance. On 12 October the 1st Battalion, Dorsetshire Regiment was in the front line at Pont Fixe, where it meets with the La Bassée Canal. The Germans launched a ferocious counter-attack and by the end of the fighting, the 1st Battalion, Dorsetshire Regiment had suffered some 420 casualties, including dead, wounded and missing.

On the first day of the Battle of the Somme, the 1st Battalion, Dorsetshire Regiment, was tasked with moving forward out of their trenches near Authuille Wood, about 5 kilometres north of Albert. By the end of that first day 69 of the battalion were dead, and by the end of the third day their casualties had increased to about 500.

Of the sixty-nine killed on that first day, including Cecil Crane, four of those men were part of 'D' Company from Poole. The other three were 22-year-old Private 15704 C.F. Young from Lytchett Matravers; Private 7643 Frank Brown, who was 41 years of age and a married man who lived at 'Kensington', Longfleet Road; and 28-year-old Sergeant 6865 Frank Jenkins, another married man, of 'Beaumont-Hamel', Wingfield Avenue, Oakdale.

There was talk early in 1916 that Germany, having not achieved a quick victory in the war as they had expected, wanted peace. This came about after the German Chancellor, Theobald von Bethmann-Hollweg, rather cleverly sent his peace proposal via the head of the Catholic Church, Pope Benedict XV, but nothing happened. Germany tried again in April 1916, reiterating the proposal and its conditions, with one of its main points being a return to pre-war boundaries, which left only Germany's overseas regions in dispute. Still nothing happened. These were uncertain times. As already stated, Germany had never foreseen the war lasting as long as it had. By the end of 1916, it had already been going on for two years and five months. The cost of continuing the war was absolutely staggering. Money was running out and food was being rationed; by the end of 1916 it was heading towards starvation levels. In terms of manpower, hundreds of thousands of men had been lost and there was not an exhaustive supply, but despite all these issues, it is possible, if not probable, that the Germans' decision to negotiate a peace was driven by fear. That fear came in the shape of America, which at this time had not yet entered the war. If the United States came into the war on the side of the allies, Germany knew that there would be absolutely no chance of a negotiated peace, and they also knew that once this happened their defeat would be inevitable.

There were those in Britain who would have taken the peace settlement. In November 1916 the 5th Marquess of Lansdowne, Henry Petty-Fitzmaurice, wrote a letter calling for a negotiated peace between Britain and Germany. The following month saw the then British Prime Minister, Herbert H. Asquith, resign, which only added to the confusion and uncertainty of the situation. His successor, David Lloyd George, had a different take on the matter. Between the beginning of the war and the end of 1916, Great Britain had lost a staggering 346,756 men who had been killed or who had died as a result of their involvement in the war. Add to this another 600,000 men who had been wounded, and that was an awful lot of men. By agreeing to a negotiated peace, David Lloyd George felt that all those casualties would have been for nothing.

At least seventy-six of those who had been killed were from Poole. Of these, fifty-five were from the army, twenty from the Royal Navy, and one from the Merchant Navy. Of these, twenty-five served with the Dorsetshire Regiment, while another served with the Dorset Yeomanry (Queen's Own).

Britain and her allies – the main one being France – didn't want a negotiated peace, they wanted an outright victory. The reasoning behind this was simple. A negotiated peace gave Germany time to recover, build up her forces and equipment once again, and come back even bigger and stronger. Lloyd George knew that he was very, very close to convincing American President Woodrow Wilson to enter the war on the side of the allies, which wasn't a foregone conclusion. At that time America had a very large German population, and in early 1917 Woodrow Wilson stated: 'We are sincere friends of the German people and earnestly desire to remain at peace with them. We shall not believe they are hostile to us unless or until we are obliged to believe it.'

On Tuesday, 5 September a meeting took place at the Guildhall of the Poole Borough Council. It was chaired by the town's mayor, Councillor George C.A. Kentish, and it was a very poignant one for the mayor. The deputy mayor, Councillor J.A. Hawkes, got the afternoon meeting up and running with a short address to all those present. He wanted to express the feelings he knew all members of the council who were present had in their hearts: their deep sympathy for the mayor and his family, and especially with Mrs Kentish, because usually the burden fell upon the mother in a time of grief. The meeting was the first time most of those at the council had seen the mayor since his loss, and he was sure that he was echoing the feelings of all present when he said that they were full of sympathy at the news of their loss. A young life cut off in the course of service and duty was both sad and tragic, and made even worse when each and every one of them knew the man concerned.

The deputy mayor said that they admired the mayor for his strength of mind and his fidelity to duty, and he passed on their collective and most heartfelt condolences. The mayor replied, thanking the councillors for their kindness and expression of sympathy. Although the report wasn't clear or precise, it was apparent that this show of sympathy was regarding a close relative they had lost in the war. George Colville Arden Kentish had been a tea-planter in India, where he lived with his wife Margaret and their daughter Enid. At the turn of the century, the Kentish family moved back to Great Britain, where they set up home in Pembrokeshire. George Kentish had obviously become a wealthy man as a tea-planter.

Grassendale boarding school for girls.

In 1908 Enid became a boarder at the Grassendale School, a prestigious boarding school for girls at Southbourne-on-Sea in Bournemouth, where she remained until 1911. On the outbreak of the Great War she began working as a nurse with the Poole section of the Voluntary Aid Detachment of the British Red Cross. Her work involved looking after the many wounded soldiers who arrived at the Cornelia Hospital in Poole. It was while doing this that she became ill and died on 18 August 1916, when she was just 22 years of age.

Somewhat surprisingly, her name is not recorded on the Commonwealth War Graves Commission website so it is not absolutely clear where she is buried, but a plaque bearing her name, Enid Margaret Kentish, can be found at St Katherine's Church at Southbourne, Bournemouth. Although Enid had been born in Bengal in India during the time her parents were living there, her sister Gwendolen was born in Pembrokeshire, Wales on 20 October 1902, soon after the family had moved back to England.

On Tuesday, 12 September an inquest took place at Parkstone into the death of 46-year-old Arthur Marsh who died at the Royal Victoria Hospital on Saturday, 9 September. He was a gardener who lived at Earlsfield, Bournemouth Road, Parkstone. Mr A.W. Malim appeared on behalf of Mr Marsh's employers, and Mr Charles F. Hiscock was in attendance on behalf of the Bournemouth Gas and Water Company, along with the company's Acting General Manager, Mr Philip G.G. Moon.

The incident leading to the death of Mr Marsh had taken place at about 7.20 am on Thursday, 7 September. Mr Marsh was cycling to work when he was involved in an encounter with a steamroller that was driven by Charles Joyce.

Mr Joyce told the inquest that he was driving his steamroller from Queen's Road into the Bournemouth Road, Parkstone at about 7.15 am on the day in question. At the time of the accident, the tail of his engine was pointing towards Bournemouth while the front of the vehicle was pointing towards Poole and his rear nearside wheel was about 18in away from the tram line just as he came to a stop. Just then he saw Mr Marsh riding his bicycle towards the rear of his steamroller and noticed that the front wheel of his bike was actually in the groove of the tram line. He saw Mr Marsh stick his hand out and put his hand on the near wheel of his steamroller to steady himself before he pushed off again, to get his front wheel out of the tram rail groove. Mr Joyce then described how, after managing to free himself from the tram line, Mr Marsh cycled across the road into the groove of the tram lines on the opposite side of the road. Mr Joyce also described how he then saw a lorry driving towards the rear of his vehicle and the bicycle that was being ridden by Mr Marsh. He described how when he first saw the lorry, it was about '48 yards away', which seemed an unusually precise distance to give.

After cycling only a short distance, Mr Marsh extricated his front wheel from the tram groove, meaning that his bike was pointing back across the road. Just at that moment the lorry struck him, knocking him down, and one of its front wheels ran over Mr Marsh. Mr Joyce estimated that the lorry was travelling at about 20 mph at the time of the accident, and he couldn't understand how the driver hadn't seen Mr Marsh on his bicycle. In response to a question about how long Mr Marsh had held on to the back of his steamroller, he said that it was for no longer than a second or two. He could not accept the suggestion that the lorry was only about 4 or 5 yards away when Mr Marsh was holding the rear of his vehicle.

Mr Charles Stokes of Bournemouth Road, Parkstone, a labourer who worked for the Poole Corporation, said he was carrying out repairs to the road when the steamroller was about 20 to 25 yards away from him. He did not see Mr Marsh approaching on his bicycle, but he did see the lorry as described by Mr Joyce and confirmed that it was travelling at about 20 mph. He looked up as the lorry passed by where he was working, and saw a man on a bicycle in the road who was heading towards Bournemouth. He did not see the actual collision between the lorry and the bicycle, but afterwards he saw a man lying on the ground.

The next to give evidence to the inquest was Mr Howard Percy House, who lived at 25 Kingston Road, Longfleet and worked as a lorry driver for the Bournemouth Gas and Water Company. At the time of the accident he was driving a 3-ton lorry which was carrying a further 3 tons in load. The speed limit for his lorry was 12 mph. As he approached Queen's Road, he noticed a steamroller backing out in the general direction of Bournemouth, at which time it was about 30 to 40 yards away from him. At about the same time he noticed a man on a bicycle riding in the groove of the tram lines, but the man hadn't at that stage reached the rear of the steam engine. Mr House continued, explaining how a short while later the man on the bicycle reached the steam engine and reached out and put his hand on the wheel to steady himself, let go and almost immediately fell down across the road, at which time Mr House was only about 4 or 5 yards away. He immediately swerved to his right, mounted the pavement to avoid running over the cyclist on the ground, and to the best of his knowledge, he did not run over the man at all. If he had done so he would have felt the bump, and a vehicle of 6-ton weight driving over anybody would have made a real mess of them physically. He braked sharply and came to a halt as soon as he could, which he estimated was within about 25 yards. Prior to braking he was travelling at about 12 mph and began slowing the more he swerved. Mr House said that he had been driving for about ten years and he had never been involved in an accident before.

Police Sergeant Miller explained that when he arrived at the scene, Mr Marsh was in a nearby house, sitting down in the living room. As he appeared to be seriously injured, Sergeant Miller immediately took him to hospital.

Dr Telford-Smith, the house surgeon at the Royal Victoria Hospital, told the inquest that Mr Marsh died at 9.30 pm on Saturday, 9 September after having been admitted on the previous Thursday. As Sergeant Miller had said, Mr Marsh had been seriously injured. He was suffering from combined fractures of the right humerus, with haemorrhaging from that as well as the fracture of several of his ribs down his right side where they joined the breastbone. The cause of death was shock due to the extent of his injuries, which were consistent with somebody having been run over by a heavy type of vehicle. In this case it could have been either the lorry or the steam engine.

Having heard all the evidence, the jury returned a verdict of 'Accidental death'. The coroner asked the foreman if they were prepared to say that the deceased man was run over by a motor lorry. The foreman replied that they would prefer to leave their verdict as 'Accidental death'.

It was announced in the local newspapers on Saturday, 14 October that Gunner 205764 Cyril William Coles, who was 23 years of age and serving with 'D' Company, No. 3 Section, Machine-Gun Corps (Heavy Branch) was killed in action on Friday, 15 September 1916. At the time of his death he was attached to an armoured car that was involved in the 'big push'. The adjutant wrote: 'Gunner C.W. Coles behaved splendidly throughout the whole action, and was liked by all at the camp.'

It is interesting how matters change over time; in this case relating to how long it took during the Great War for the announcement of the loss of Gunner Coles. It was a month after his death before his demise was finally announced in the newspapers. He was buried at the Bull Road Cemetery, Flers in the Somme region.

Gunner Coles had been heavily involved with the Poole Congregational Church before enlisting in the army, and had played a full part in the church's general social work in the parish. His father, Mr William Clement Coles, lived at 'Stoneleigh', Wimborne Road, Poole, although the 1911 census showed the family home being at Creek Moor Mill, near Poole with Mr Coles, his wife Sarah Ann, Cyril and their other son Donald Durant Coles, who was two years younger than Cyril.

Cyril was 18 years of age at the time and is shown as working in a corn still, apparently connected to his father's work as a miller and corn merchant. Donald also served during the Great War, having enlisted on 30 September 1915 at Bournemouth as a Private (M2/130809) in the 595th Motor Transport Company, Army Service Corps, at the age of 20. Some of his service saw him deployed as an 'Ambulance Car Driver', which was in keeping with his work in civilian life as a chauffeur.

His army service record shows that he was in England between 30 September and 23 October 1915. Then he became part of the Mediterranean Expeditionary Force between 24 October 1915 and 19 February 1917. From 20 February to 5 December 1917 he was stationed in Malta, then finally he boarded a ship on 6 December 1917 en route to England as an invalid, but there was no reason given for this and no clarification as to whether he had been wounded or was suffering from illness or disease. He arrived at his destination on 17 December 1917, remained at home for the rest of the war and was finally demobbed on 28 February 1919.

On Saturday, 4 November a meeting took place of the Dorset County Appeal Tribunal at Poole Guildhall, with Mr J.C. Swinburne Hanham presiding. Other members who made up the tribunal were Sir George Ruthven C. Hunte, Mr H. Bradley, Mr G. Profiet, Mr H. Paverly, Captain Chubb, the military representative, and Mr R. Arnold from the Board of Agriculture. Mr Jackson was in attendance as the clerk.

Mr Archibald H. Yeatman asked that in the case of Thomas William Sidnell, who was a cinema house proprietor of Swanage, if it was possible for the man to have another hearing on the grounds of financial hardship. Mr Sidnell had previously been granted conditional exemption by the Swanage tribunal and Captain Chubb had appealed against that decision, the appeal being allowed from 15 December 1916. If the tribunal would give their consent for Mr Sidnell to be given a further hearing, Mr Yeatman said that he could bring further evidence, some of it from the police, that it was desirable that the cinema should be allowed to continue in operation as it was a deterrent in preventing soldiers from wandering the streets of the towns in which they were billeted late at night. Sadly for Mr Sidnell, Mr Yeatman's application on his behalf was disallowed.

Mr A.J. Lawman of Bournemouth asked that the case of Albert James Bartlett, who was 41 years of age and an oil and hardware merchant, be adjourned until Parliament had finally settled the position of a man who had already reached this age. Mr Bartlett had turned 41 on 3 July 1916, was an unattested man and had been granted exemption until 15 December by the Poole rural tribunal. The case was adjourned to the next sitting so that Mr Bartlett could undergo a medical examination to ascertain whether his level of fitness was suitable.

Mr Lawman was also making an application on behalf of Sidney James Smith, a pawnbroker from Branksome who had previously been granted one month's exemption by the Poole borough tribunal. Mr Lawman told the members of the tribunal that the case had previously been before the appeals tribunal and was adjourned for the purpose of Smith producing books to show his business turnover. Mr Lawman then produced the books on behalf of Smith for the members to peruse. Once they had done so they granted him a five-month exemption until 31 March 1917.

George William Loveless, 34 years of age, was a single man who worked as an electrician at the Picture House, Winton. He appealed for a further exemption on the grounds of domestic hardship. He stated that the case had been before the Poole rural tribunal several times, and the members who sat on it admitted that his was a difficult case to deal with. Loveless was the sole supporter of his invalid mother. He was granted a conditional exemption, as long as his mother's condition remained as it was, and that he obtained work of national importance.

Mr Yeatman represented 29-year-old married man Mr Frank Samuel Lovell of Yarrells Farm, Lytchett Minster, even though the application on behalf of Mr Lovell had been brought before the panel by his father, Mr John Lovell. The appeal was against an earlier decision made by the Poole rural tribunal which had disallowed his application on the grounds that there would be no case of 'hardship' if the man was called up. Mr Yeatman informed the panel that Lovell was the only man left on the farm. The appeal was adjourned from 15 November, which meant that Lovell would have to enlist in the army on that date.

Messrs Bacon and Curtis of Poole appealed in the case of Herbert George Huey Cobb, a married man who was 29 years of age and lived at 32 Hill Street, Poole. He was a coppersmith, plumber and sheet metal worker who had been granted a month's exemption, but with the caveat that there was no leave for any further appeal. Mr Frank Bacon appeared in support of the appeal for Cobb, and said that the firm had already lost a great many men and that it was impossible to replace such skilled workers. The appeal was dismissed as of 31 December.

Mr George H. Bailey was the appellant against the decision of the Poole borough tribunal in the case of George Cobb, who was a single man, aged 21, who lived at 'Oakdale', Longfleet, Poole. He was an agricultural labourer, to whom one month's exemption had been granted with no further application without leave. Mr Yeatman appeared in front of the tribunal in support of the appeal, but it was dismissed from 31 December.

Mr Bailey also made a similar application for his own son, Percy George Bailey, who was 20 years old, a single man who worked as a market gardener and lived at Bushill Mill, Longfleet. The original application was heard at the Poole borough tribunal and had been disallowed. The grounds for that application are unknown, but it was appealing that decision that had resulted in them coming before the county tribunal. The appeal was disallowed.

Having been granted three months' exemption by the Poole borough tribunal, Frederick Cecil Fox, a married man who was 32 years of age and lived at 84 High Street, Poole and was a hairdresser, appealed against the borough tribunal's decision. The appeal was allowed, with an exemption being granted until 31 December. This was somewhat strange as there was no explanation as to why the appeal was allowed. Certainly being a hairdresser wasn't a reserved occupation of national importance, and there was no mention of financial hardship or any family-related dependency.

Walter Cross was 39 years of age, a married man who lived at 20 Heckford Road, Poole and was what passed in 1916 as a taxi driver. He was initially granted a period of two months exemption on the condition that he did not lodge another claim without consent. Despite this, he decided to appeal against that decision. The appeal was dismissed from 31 December.

It appeared that he was doing everything within his power to avoid enlisting in the army.

Messrs W.H. Yeatman and Sons Ltd of the High Street, Poole had placed an application before the tribunal in relation in relation to Arthur George Pointer, who was 27 years of age, a married man of 'Daisy Mead', Sandbourne Road, Poole. He worked as a buyer and manager of a shop that was situated in the High Street, Poole. He was also the sole cashier and book-keeper, to whom the Poole borough tribunal had granted a three months' exemption with no renewal without consent, and he had to serve with the Poole section of the Volunteer Training Corps. The appeal was dismissed.

Mr R. Lester of the Refuge Assurance Company was appealing on behalf of Joseph Tuck against a decision of the Poole borough tribunal. Tuck was 40 years of age and a married man who lived at 'Tintangel', Poole. His position at the company was one of superintendent. He had been granted one month's exemption, but on this occasion his appeal was adjourned to allow time for Tuck to undergo a thorough medical examination to ascertain if he was physically fit enough for wartime military service.

Mr A. Carter, 25 years of age and working as a contractor and haulier, was a married man of Fancy Road, Newton. He was appealing against the decision of the Poole borough tribunal, which had granted him a one-month exemption on the condition that he would not apply again without consent. The appeal was, not surprisingly, dismissed.

Mr Yeatman, who was having a busy day at the tribunal, also appeared on behalf of William Walter George Blandford, who was 36 years of age and a married man who lived at and was the licensee of the Globe Hotel, High Street, Poole. The Poole borough tribunal had twice previously granted Mr Blandford two three-month periods of exemption, the last one being on condition that he made no further such applications without permission to do so. His appeal, which was before the tribunal on the grounds of hardship, was dismissed.

Albert William Mullins of Oakley Cottage, Uppleby Road, Parkstone was in the joint employ of Doctor Tuthill and

Doctor Gray Edwards as a chauffeur and mechanic who had been granted three months' exemption by the Poole borough tribunal, subject to no further claims being lodged without leave. However, he wasn't before the county tribunal because he wanted to appeal that decision, he was there because the military authorities had appealed the decision. The two doctors, via Mr H.F.W. Gwatkin, also lodged an appeal and asked for a further exemption. Having considered the merits of the case, the tribunal members dismissed the military's appeal and allowed the one made by the two doctors, but only until 31 December.

Mr Yeatman appeared on behalf of Mr Thomas Cole of 'Merrington', Longfleet, Poole who was a government subcontractor to appeal against a decision made by the Poole borough tribunal in relation to two of his workers: Mr William George Toop, who was 29 years of age and a married man of Amity Cottages, Poole, employed as a foreman carter of English timber; and Gilbert Golding, who was 25 years of age, married and living at 3 Avenue Building, Poole, a carter of English timber. The Poole borough tribunal had disallowed Golding's application and exempted Toop for one month. Since then Toop had been badged by the Ministry of Munitions, an application for the badge had been lodged prior to the appeal, and this appeal had been adjourned indefinitely. In Golding's case the appeal was dismissed from 15 November.

Mr Trevanion appeared on behalf of Messrs May and Hassall who were timber merchants. They were appealing against the decision of the Poole borough tribunal in the case of one of their workers, Lionel Stoddart Milledge, who was 33 years of age and lived at Marnhull Road, Poole and was employed as a timber merchant's surveyor. He had been granted a final one month's exemption on the grounds that he did not apply again without leave to do so. The appeal was allowed, with an exemption put in place until 31 March 1917.

There were then two cases in which the military authorities appealed the earlier decisions made by the Poole borough tribunal. The first was that of Arthur Harold Newman, who was 20 years of age, was the house porter at the Branksome

Towers Hotel and had been granted three months' exemption. The appeal was allowed and the certificate of exemption was withdrawn as of 15 November. The second case involved a William Fagg, who was 18 years of age, a single man who had not attested and who lived at 19 Market Street, Poole. He was a baker and had been granted a four-month exemption. In his case, the appeal was dismissed.

Mr Dodham appeared on behalf of Harold Wilford Eaves, a youthful painter who lived at 'Devonia', Leyton Road, Upper Parkstone. The man had claimed exemption at the Poole borough tribunal on the grounds of being a conscientious objector to military service. It was subsequently discovered that he had served with the Territorials prior to the outbreak of the war, which led the local tribunal to disbelieve his claim of being a bona fide conscientious objector. In the circumstances the only exemption he was provided with was the requirement to have to undertake combatant service. He had twice previously gone before the appeals tribunal. On the first occasion the appeal was dismissed and the decision of the Poole borough tribunal was upheld. The second application was in the form of a leave for a re-hearing in order that evidence might be brought to prove that domestic hardship would result from him being made to enlist for military service. Consent for a re-hearing was approved, and Mr Dodham appeared to support the case on those grounds. After the case had been heard, the tribunal also refused to believe his claim to being a genuine conscientious objector, also stating that the case of domestic hardship had not been proven, and the appeal was dismissed.

It was interesting to note that eighteen men from the Poole area had, for a number of different reasons, claimed exemptions from having to undergo military training; a similar number to those from the Poole area who were enlisting each day.

On 9 December, it was announced that Sergeant Walter Hugh Victor Mackintosh, who was born on 12 April 1888 in Poole, the fourth son of the late Doctor Henry Mackintosh and Ellen Mackintosh, had been awarded the Military Medal for bravery in the field. He had enlisted as a Private (55109) in the 2nd Battalion, Canadian Overseas Expeditionary Force on 9 November 1914 in Toronto. He later transferred to the 19th Battalion of the same unit and was promoted to the rank of sergeant on 1 March 1915.

At the time of the announcement, Sergeant Mackintosh was still a patient at Highfield Hall Hospital at Southampton, where he had been admitted on 17 October 1916 having been severely wounded in the action that led to him being awarded his medal. Along with his colleagues he was involved in fighting at the Battle of Courcelette on 15 September 1916. At the time he was in charge of a company of men from his battalion. During the initial advance he was shot through the left arm in two places, causing a fracture. Soon afterwards a stretcher-bearer cleaned and dressed his wounds and Sergeant Mackintosh moved on, but when only a few yards away from the German trenches he was struck in the right arm by a piece of shrapnel from an exploding artillery shell, resulting in a compound fracture. While lying on the ground, trying to regain his thoughts after being knocked over by the blast of the explosion, he was also shot through the side. He had previously been wounded in the head and shoulder during fighting at St Eloi on 11 April 1916.

On 4 May 1916, Walter Mackintosh was the subject of a medical board examination that took place at a Red Cross hospital at Ramsgate. The findings of that examination were as follows:

> September 15/16: there are now limitations in the movement of his right elbow, wrist and shoulder. Very slight discharge in a wound in the right upper arm. Physical condition otherwise excellent. Was boarded to be invalided to Canada, but the man states that he feels able to carry on with instructional or other base-related duties and the Board recommends that he be given the chance to do so for 2 to 3 months before a review of his physical condition.

He must have subsequently recovered sufficiently to be returned to active duty because on 14 February 1918, he was wounded yet again when he sustained a gunshot wound to his right elbow and wrist, which saw him spend time in both the No. 11 and No. 5 Canadian General Hospitals before being invalided back to Canada on 6 May 1918. Walter was subsequently medically discharged from the Canadian army on 15 March 1919 as unfit for military service.

CHAPTER FOUR

1917: Seeing it Through

As the war moved into its fourth year, David Lloyd George had made Britain's direction in the war very clear indeed. There was absolutely nothing ambiguous about his intentions. Put plain and simple, by rejecting Germany's offer of a negotiated peace, he was saying in no uncertain terms that he wanted victory at all costs, no matter what the price was, either in lives or financially.

This was a decision that would have a direct effect on Poole, because between 1 January 1917 and 11 November 1918, at least 126 men from Poole were killed or died in the war. Even when the Armistice was signed and the fighting came to an end, the dying didn't stop. Between 11 November 1918 and 19 May 1920, there were another eleven men from Poole who died of their wounds sustained during the war or from illness or disease.

One of those killed was 21-year-old Frederick George Poole, a Private (14675) serving with the 1st Battalion, Dorsetshire Regiment. He is buried at the Longuenesse Souvenir Cemetery at St Omer in the Pas-de-Calais region of France. He had previously served as Private 19915 with the Duke of Cornwall Light Infantry before transferring to the Dorsetshire Regiment. His parents, Frederick and Annie Poole, lived at 58 Garland Road, Heckford Park, Longfleet. At the time of the 1911 census, they were living there with their eight children, including Frederick. There were four daughters – Annie, the eldest, Winnie, Doris and Kate – along with their three other sons, Charles, James and Arthur.

The first big event of 1917 in military terms was Germany's announcement that she was to resume her policy of unrestricted submarine warfare, which meant that her U-boats would sink on sight any allied vessels they came across. This policy began on 1 February 1917.

On 12 March Russian troops mutinied in Petrograd, and three days later Tsar Nicholas II abdicated.

America finally entered the conflict on 6 April 1917, when President Woodrow Wilson declared war on Germany. Throughout the months of April, May and June, unrest spread throughout the French army as troops showed their disgust at their military leaders' barbaric tactics of head-on attacks into heavily-defended enemy positions, resulting in the loss of tens of thousands of French lives.

The worst single incident of British civilian casualties of the Great War took place on 17 June when German aircraft bombed London, resulting in 583 casualties, 158 of whom were killed.

Three and a half months after declaring war on Germany, American troops arrived in France for the first time on 25 June.

The Battle of Passchendaele began on 31 July and saw Belgian, British and French troops take on German forces. It continued for three months, one week and three days, before finally coming to an end on 10 November. Allied casualties for the battle have been a point of conjecture for many years and estimates have varied between 200,000 and 448,618. Similar variations for German casualties also exist.

The Battle of Cambrai began on 20 November and ended two weeks later on 4 December. It included the use of the largest number of tanks by the British in one battle throughout the entire war. By the end of the battle the British had lost 179 of the 476 tanks they had thrown into the fight, while sustaining some 40,000 casualties.

As the year drew to a close, December saw a couple of big events. Firstly, and after some prolonged and at times fierce fighting, British forces finally wrestled Jerusalem from Turkish control on 9 December. On 15 December Russia and Germany signed an Armistice and just one week later peace talks began at Brest-Litovsk.

Spread throughout the year's events, Poole lost somewhere in the region of seventy men who had been killed in the different theatres of war. This included the death of one of the town's very own. This came in the shape of Private 14675 Frederick George Poole, who was 21 years of age when he was killed in action on 24 June.

On the afternoon of Sunday, 14 January 1917, a large crowd of spectators gathered to watch the 200-strong 'A' (Poole) Company of the Dorset Volunteer Regiment, under the command of Lieutenant S. Archer Phillips, muster and carry out drill and other manoeuvres before they were inspected at Poole Park by General Sir Henry Crichton Sclater, the commanding officer of the Southern Command. Besides the presence of other military 'bigwigs', the mayor of Poole, Councillor Kentish, was also in attendance.

After the inspection, General Sclater delivered a short address to the men, telling them that what they had done and were doing was appreciated not just by the people of Poole, but by the entire country. The nation's people were also watching to see when their patriotism was going to step forward and join the defence forces of the country and be ready in an emergency. The general said he hoped they would bear in mind that a possible invasion by German forces was not a fairy tale. In his experience it was usually the unexpected aspects in war that generally occurred, and at any moment they and he might be called upon to defend their hearths and homes. He explained how the War Office, via the army, was keen to assist them in their training, which needed to include rifle-shooting, bomb-throwing, bayonet-fighting and trench warfare. He hoped that by the time he next inspected them, not only would their numbers have increased but the level of their training would be in line with the technicalities of modern warfare.

General Sclater was an experienced officer. Having first been commissioned in the Royal Artillery in 1875, he went on to serve as a deputy assistant adjutant general at the headquarters of the

Nile expedition between 1884 and 1885. He was promoted to the rank of major on 15 June 1885 and soon after he served in the Egyptian Frontier Field Force between 1885 and 1886. He also served in the Second Boer War, after which Lord Kitchener, who was the commander-in-chief of British Forces in South Africa, wrote the following about him in a despatch dated June 1902: 'Sclater possesses an unusual combination of ability and common sense. I consider him to be a staff officer of exceptional value to whom all ranks of the Royal Artillery in South Africa owe much.'

In 1902 Sclater accompanied Lord Roberts, commander-in-chief of British Forces, and St John Brodrick, Secretary of State for War, on a visit to Germany as a guest of the Emperor Wilhelm to attend and observe German army manoeuvres. He worked at the War Office as the Director of Artillery between 1903 and 1904 before serving in India as the commander of the Quetta Division in 1908. During the Great War between 1914 and 1916 he was a member of the Army Council, and between 1916 and 1919 he was the general officer commanding for Southern Command before retiring in 1922, having served in the British army for forty-seven years. He died the following year aged 67. It must have been a great experience for the members of the Poole Company of the Dorset Volunteer Regiment to have been inspected by such an experienced and well-respected soldier.

On Thursday, 8 February the Poole Police Court saw Reginald Bunker, a sergeant in the army, summonsed for driving a motor cycle without lights at Longfleet on 30 January 1916. Sergeant Bunker told the court that the lights on his motor cycle went out when he reached the top of the hill and there was bright moonlight that had lit up the skyline. The roads were empty with nobody else about, or nobody that he could see. He rode slowly down the hill before turning into Shaftesbury Road and was trimming the lamps when he bumped into a policeman on his patrol.

Mayor Councillor Kentish, who was chairman of the bench, said that they did not wish to endorse the defendant's licence, and the case was demised on payment of 2s 6d in court costs, but Sergeant Bunker was also summonsed for failing to produce his driving licence, which he told the court he had found in his jacket pocket when he got home. His explanation was accepted by the court and the summons was dismissed.

On Sunday, 4 March a soldier from Poole had a memorial dedicated in his name at St Mary's Church, Longfleet during the evening service by the Reverend W. Okes Parish, in the shape of 'Glastonbury Chair'. The soldier in question was Private 29676 Sidney Arthur Cave of the 2nd Battalion, Hampshire Regiment, who was one of the tens of thousands killed during the Battle of the Somme when he died on Wednesday, 18 October 1916. Sadly, like many of them, he has no known grave as his body was never recovered; instead, his name is commemorated on the Thiepval Memorial in the Somme region of France.

The dedication took place at the lectern, where it had been placed for convenience, with the choir and other members of the clergy singing the hymn *Lead us, heavenly Father, lead us.* Canon Parish chose to read the sixth verse of Psalm 12 from the Bible, 'The righteous shall be had in remembrance.' He then remarked how he knew that the service of dedication would have different meaning for each and every person present. He told of the special meaning it had for him, as he had baptized Sidney Arthur Cave as a baby and had then helped prepare him for his confirmation in the Catholic Church, since which time he had been a 'good son' in the faith of the church, and he had looked forward to the day when he would unite him in wedlock with the woman of his affections. Sadly that was not to be. The 'Glastonbury Chair', he said, reminded them all of brave men who went off to fight in the war and were killed. Speaking again of Private Sidney Cave, he told how when he initially enlisted in the army, he served with the Dorsets before being transferred to the Hampshire Regiment, with whom he was serving when he was killed in action. Canon Parish said that he was quite certain Private Sidney Cave would forever more be held in the hearts of the people of Poole with grateful remembrance. This is perhaps an interesting aspect of the war; that such remembrance services took place throughout the years of the fighting, rather than just springing up once it was all over.

Saturday, 21 April highlighted not only how cruel the war could be, but just how far its tentacles could reach. Hubert Skinner wasn't a soldier serving in the war but he was, at 56 years of age, remarkably still an Able Seaman (98795) in the Royal Navy, serving as part of the crew of HMS *Osborne*. He hadn't been hurt or injured in a Zeppelin raid, but with his wife dead and his four sons all having enlisted in the army and serving in France, life sadly became too much for him to deal with. Aged 56, he was found dead in his home at 3 Stanley Cottages, Wimborne Road, Poole. He had hung himself.

The inquest into his death took place on the afternoon of Monday, 23 April at the Guildhall in Poole, in front of the Borough Coroner, Mr F.J. Conway. Sidney had been identified by his sister, Mrs Jane Hooper of 2 Ashley Cottages, High Street, Poole, who told the inquest that he was at home on leave from his ship that was stationed in South Wales. He had visited her on the Friday, the day before his death, and he had been in good spirits and his health appeared fine. She had been expecting him for breakfast on the Saturday morning, but he never showed up. As the day continued and she still hadn't heard from him, she decided to go to his home where she arrived at around 3.00 pm. She let herself in and called out to him, but received no reply. She went upstairs, entered his bedroom and found him hanging on the back of the door. He had evidently been in bed, as he was dressed in his pants and shirt. She had found a 'suicide note' which she recognized was in his handwriting and was of a farewell nature. He had never spoken to her about having any suicidal thoughts, but he had worried since losing his wife Julia who had died in May 1915, and about his four sons who were all serving in France.

Doctor W.T. Gardiner Robinson attended at 3 Stanley Cottages, Wimborne Road, Poole on the day in question, arriving there around 4.00 pm. He went upstairs and saw that Hubert Skinner was dead and rigid, with a deep purple mark around his neck in keeping with the wounds caused by the rope with which he had hung himself. There were also marks around his wrists, and the doctor estimated that death had occurred some twelve hours earlier, putting it at about four o'clock that morning. Doctor Robinson also noticed a chair lying on its side in the middle of the room, which had evidently been what Hubert Skinner had been standing on before pushing it away. He had always known the deceased as a good, steady-going man, who had been a cheerful soul whenever they had met.

Police Constable Blues told the inquest that he had been called to Hubert Skinner's home and when he arrived, he found the deceased hanging by his neck on the back of the bedroom door; his feet were tied with a piece of string and his hands, which were behind his back, had been constricted with a lanyard. Even though he knew Skinner was dead, he cut him down and laid him on his bed. Like Doctor Robinson, Constable Blues had also known the deceased as a steady and cheerful individual. The jury returned a verdict of death due to strangulation by Hubert Skinner hanging himself in a fit of temporary insanity.

A check of the Royal Navy and Royal Marine War Graves Roll, 1914–1919, shows that he was buried at the Hamworthy Churchyard, near Poole. More interestingly, though, it shows his cause of death as 'Died from disease'. Maybe this was an act of kindness by the authorities in trying to hide the fact that he had committed suicide. Hubert and Julia's four sons were Percy, Hubert, Arthur and Stanley, the latter of which the author knows served as a Gunner (13505) in the Royal Marine Artillery.

May 1917 brought with it a spectrum of war-related news for the residents of Poole. Some of it was good and, sadly, some of it wasn't.

Between the latter part of 1914, when the first military patients arrived at the Grata Quies Auxiliary Hospital at Branksome Park, and May 1917, there had been in the region of 850 sick and wounded British and Belgian soldiers treated there. Somewhat remarkably, there had not been one single death until Monday, 21 May when Private (17020) Albert Edward Garland became the first soldier to die there. It could be said that he literally came home to die, as he was originally from Branksome where his wife and children were living at the time of his death.

He was badly wounded while fighting in France, before being sent home for treatment. Originally he was sent to the Mont Dore Military Hospital at Bourne Avenue, Bournemouth, which prior to being requisitioned as a military hospital had been the Mont Dore Hotel. When it ceased being used as a military hospital in 1919, it did not return to being a hotel; instead it became the Bournemouth Town Hall, which is still its function today. Private Garland was subsequently transferred to the Grata Quies Auxiliary Hospital, where he passed away after his health deteriorated dramatically in the days leading up to his death.

His funeral took place on Thursday, 24 May at Branksome Cemetery, Poole. A number of wounded soldiers who were patients at the Grata Quies attended, and the hospital sent a floral tribute. A detachment of soldiers, including a firing party, also attended, and the coffin was borne on a gun carriage. A large crowd gathered at the cemetery to see Albert Garland being laid to rest.

Mrs W. Harvey of West Shore, Poole received news that her youngest brother, Private H. Lock, had been awarded the Military Medal. He was himself a native of Poole, and had previously worked for the London and South Western Railway Company, but in the months leading up to the outbreak of the Great War, he emigrated to Canada and acquired a job working for the Great Pacific Railway. With the war under way, he enlisted in the Canadian army and after his initial training was sent out to France with the second contingent of Canadians, being attached to the 4th Field Ambulance with whom he had served since 1915. He had two brothers who served in the British army during the war.

Mrs Sarah Cutler, previously of West Street, Poole, had five sons serving in the British army. Charles Cutler was a Private (55032) in the 193rd Company, Machine-Gun Corps, when he was killed in action on Sunday, 15 April while serving in France. He was buried at the Mont-Huon Military Cemetery at Le Tréport in the Seine-Maritime region of France. He was 26 years of age and a married man, whose widow, at the end of the war, was living at 6 Palmerston Row, West Street, Poole.

Her husband, George Cutler, had died in 1904, but she did not remarry. Her four other sons all survived the war. George Cutler, who was 23 years of age, had served and then been medically discharged from the army for no longer being physically fit for wartime military service. Lance Corporal Walter Cutler, who was 36 years of age and Sarah Cutler's eldest son, served with the Sherwood Foresters (Notts & Derby Regiment), and first arrived in France in 1915. Bombardier Frank Cutler, who was 33 years of age, served with the Royal Field Artillery, and had also been in France since 1915. Last but by no means least was Albert E. Cutler, and despite being only 21 years of age, he had already reached the rank of sergeant and served with the RAMC. Like his brothers Frank and Walter, he had also first arrived in France in 1915.

On the afternoon of Saturday, 19 May Brigadier General Cayley inspected the Poole Company, Dorset Volunteer Regiment at Dane Court, Parkstone. The company turned out some eighty men for the inspection, under the watchful eye of Lieutenant S. Archer Phillips, for the visit of their distinguished visitor and greeted him with a general salute. Brigadier General Cayley addressed both the officers and men, telling them that he had heard a great deal about the splendid patrol work that they had done and continued to do, and of the patriotism they displayed in undertaking these duties. He congratulated them on this work and for the smartness of their turnout before him. At the request of the brigadier general, the men formed into squads in order that he might see how they trained. This included them displaying their bombing and bayonet-fighting skills for his inspection. When finished, he stated that he was suitably impressed.

June 1917 saw Mrs Rogers of Layton Road, Upper Parkstone a very proud mother when she received the news that both of her sons had been awarded the Military Medal for their bravery while serving in France. Private H. Rogers of the Dorsetshire Regiment had served in France since the outbreak of the war, and had taken part in every engagement in which his regiment had been involved. Sergeant F.G. Rogers left England in July 1916 as a private for active service in France and was subsequently promoted.

On Wednesday, 13 June a meeting took place in the Church House, Parkstone, under the auspices of the Territorial Force,

Brigadier General Cayley.

to consider the proposal of a field ambulance for the borough of Poole. In the absence of the mayor, Councillor Kentish, the meeting was presided over by Doctor Tuthill, who spoke of the importance of ambulance work and the number of lives an effective service could save. The secretary of the Territorial Forces County Association, Colonel R.H. Simmonds, told the meeting that it was desired to raise two ambulances in Dorset. The town of Weymouth was well under way with its preparation for such a vehicle, and as Dorchester could not, for different reasons, undertake the same commitment, it was decided that the next large town, which just happened to be Poole, would be approached to see what the response would be. Colonel Simmonds was keen to discover, if Poole did in fact raise enough funding to purchase such an ambulance, how that would interfere with the local Voluntary Aid Detachment and the work they did. He was of the opinion that it would help rather than hinder. Colonel Simmonds alluded to the transformation that had taken place since the early days, going back to 1878, when the volunteer movement had been belittled by the government and so-called experts of the day, but throughout the Great War in which men were killed and wounded on an almost industrial scale, they had more than showed their worth to both the military and civilian authorities.

In case of an invasion by the Germans which, admittedly, became less likely the longer the war continued but was still a real possibility, the formation of a Field Ambulance Corps for home use was most definitely the right way to go. There would be two sections. Section A was for men over the age of 41, who would sign an undertaking for the whole period of the war, and as a member of the corps every man would be supplied with a free uniform. Section B was for younger men who were ineligible for military service or had been exempted by military tribunals, but being in the corps would not protect them from being called up if their reason for being exempt or ineligible changed.

Colonel Simmonds had seen in the Press the call by men over military age to be allowed to play their part. By joining the corps, here was, he said, the very chance they were talking about and looking for. Everything possible that could be done to increase the number and efficiency of those men still at home, for whatever reason, meant that more men could be released to enlist in the army and go to fight. Should the corps be called upon to do anything in the event of a German invasion of the nation, its members should be prepared and willing to go and work anywhere in the United Kingdom. In Dorset, a motor transport section had been formed and the number of car-owners who were willing to provide their vehicles for official use was more than 300 which, the colonel suggested, showed that things were moving in the right direction.

On the evening of Monday, 9 July a meeting took place at the Poole Guildhall to discuss the question of the erection of a memorial for the town, to the memory of men from Poole who had been killed and those who would be killed before the war was at an end. Mayor Councillor Kentish said that at a recent meeting of the Borough Council, he had brought up the subject of such a memorial and he had been asked by his colleagues to form a committee to look into the matter further. He had called upon others to join the committee, including the sheriff and Alderman Ballard, and between them they had decided to invite to a meeting all the town's aldermen, the senior councillor of each ward, along with the clergy and ministers of the town's churches. They had all been invited, the mayor said, so that it would make their opinion more widely known, get the townsfolk to take more interest in the idea, and hopefully come up with some good ideas about what their memorial should look like.

Since he had called the meeting, all the local newspapers had agreed to come on board with the idea and include articles in their future editions about the proposed memorial. The mayor suggested they should form themselves into a general committee, and from that they should then elect an executive committee of eight or nine, which he felt would be a sufficient number. A discussion was needed, he said, as to whether they should begin canvassing views while the war was still being waged or wait until it was over regarding what form the proposed memorial should take. The mayor added that some months earlier, he had written a letter that appeared in the local Press asking the relatives of men who had fallen in the war to send him their names and particulars, but sadly he did not receive a single reply.

The trouble with such meetings and committees is that the more people are involved, the more opinions and ideas come out of it, which isn't always helpful as quite often individuals become entrenched in the belief that their idea is the best and they refuse to allow for any movement or flexibility in their stance. This meeting proved to be no different, with disagreement being the order of the day. Alderman Julyan, Councillor Hoare, Councillor Hogg and Alderman Ballard all came up with sensible yet differing suggestions as to the way forward. Possibly the suggestion that provoked most discussion was that of Councillor Cole, who said that he felt quite strongly on the matter. They had, he suggested, been called together to show some public expression to the men of the town who were involved in the actual fighting, as it was they who were making the real sacrifices. He continued that before they as a committee did anything in the way of ordering or commissioning any stonework, they should see that proper provision was made for the wounded and the relatives of those who had already been killed in the fighting.

The mayor asked Councillor Cole if he was going to move to an amendment. Councillor Cole replied that was what he had just done, to which the mayor countered that it wasn't. Councillor Cole then began speaking, when the mayor interrupted him: 'Excuse me Councillor Cole, I can run this meeting.' To this the councillor replied: 'I know you can; get on with it.'

Councillor Green entered the affray on the side of Councillor Cole, saying that he felt there should be a town meeting on the matter to which all the townsfolk should be invited. The mayor agreed that it was a matter for the town as a whole to decide. He saw their meeting as simply coming up with suggestions, none of which were binding in any way whatsoever. There was much discussion about which direction should be taken, with the general consensus being that despite whatever committee or subcommittee they raised, a public meeting needed to be called on the subject so that the town's people could have their say before any decisions were made about the way forward.

It had clearly been a meeting that had raised passionate and heartfelt discussion among those present. After all, it was an extremely important decision as how best to commemorate those men from Poole who had given their lives in defence of the nation. This most certainly wasn't a decision that could or should be made by the town's dignitaries on their own without any consultation with the town's residents, especially those families who had lost loved ones.

On Wednesday, 29 August a session of the Poole Police Court took place at Branksome, the bench being made up of Mayor Councillor Kentish, Mr J.J. Norton, Dr Montgomery and Councillor Mr W.P. Hunt. The day started off with the case of Mr Edward Derrick, a 46-year-old married man who worked as a general labourer and lived at 5 Archway Road, Branksome, who had been summoned to appear before the court for being drunk on licensed premises. When all the evidence had been heard, it was determined by the bench that the case was proven, Mr Derrick was found guilty and ordered to pay a fine of 10s plus 5s in costs.

According to the 1911 census, Edward and his wife Annie had three daughters: Edith, Annie and Nora. Since their marriage in 1898, Annie had actually given birth to six children, but three of them had died. One of them, George, who was born in 1900, had died in late 1908, when he was 8 years of age.

The next three cases were all lighting order prosecutions, two of which involved members of the public, one of whom failed to attend the hearing in response to the summons that had been issued against her, and the third involved the Branksome Towers Hotel. In each case the witnesses were members of the Poole Volunteer Training Corps who had been on night-time foot patrol duties. All three cases were proven, and those concerned were fined either 5s or £1.

During the Great War it was not permitted to have a naked light visible from a window or doorway of a house during the hours of darkness. It was a very dangerous thing to do as it could make the property concerned and any surrounding premises vulnerable and a potential target for an attacking German Zeppelin or naval vessel.

The next case before the court that day was a particularly sad one, and what would today be referred to as a case of domestic violence. Charles Smart of Shelbourne Road, Malmesbury Park and late of Dunsford Road, Upper Parkstone was summoned by his wife, Mary Jane Smart, for desertion. She told the court that they had been married for twenty-four years, during which time there had been a great deal of what she referred to as 'quarrelling'. She said that on Sunday, 12 August, he had taken an iron out of her hand and bruised her. He then threw all of the clothes that she had ironed out into the street and placed the still hot iron on her hand, causing a mild burn. Not satisfied with that, he then grabbed hold of her hair so tightly that he pulled some of it out by the roots.

On Sunday, 13 August Charles Smart left the matrimonial home, leaving his wife without any money and on Friday,

17 August he returned to the home while she was at work and removed the best part of the furniture. Three of the couple's eight children still lived at home, and it was for this reason that Mrs Smart asked for a separation order against her husband and for the custody of her three youngest children.

Mr C.G. Trevanion, Mrs Smart's solicitor, told the court that Mr Smart's allegations against his wife were not true, i.e. that she had allowed her children to be out wandering and playing in the streets until 10.30 pm, nor had she stayed out until 1.00 am. She did once enter a public house and left her child outside, but only to go in to get a bottle of stout. She pawned one of her children's boots, but only to get enough money to be able to purchase food for the children. Mr Trevanion said that it was also not true, as Mr Smart claimed, that he was paying his wife 24s a week for the children's wellbeing. The only money that she had coming into the home was the 13 shillings that two of her children earned in wages. He admitted that she had been charged with being drunk and incapable, but claimed that this had only happened because she had not eaten for some time prior to having consumed the alcohol. Mrs Smart once had as many as twenty pawn tickets, and her husband had once gone to the pawnbrokers and told them not to allow her to pledge any more items. She denied her husband's claim that because she spent so much money on drink, he took over the finances from her so that he could get the children some boots.

Mrs Love Lee, a neighbour of the Smarts, told the court that she saw Mrs Smart throwing things outside her gate and heard Mr Smart telling his wife to clear out, which she had heard him say to her on many occasions. She also told the court that she had seen him knock his wife to the floor on many occasions and had heard her scream out when he had done so. On one occasion she had seen Mrs Smart outside her home with her hair down and blood coming from her mouth. She had seen Mr Smart drunk on many occasions but never Mrs Smart, although she knew she did take a drink now and again.

Mrs Lee described to the court how it was difficult for any of the neighbours to sleep when Mr Smart was 'on with his little games'. She added that he acted like a mad man, and when he did, there were not many who would intervene. Another neighbour, Frances Ellen, said that Mrs Smart kept her children and her home looking very clean. Mr Trevanion submitted that Mr Smart had done all that he possibly could to try to stop his wife from drinking, and that there had been a contribution of 32s per week to the 'common fund'.

Nellie Smart, one of the older children who no longer lived at home, told the court that she had never seen her father strike her mother with an iron or pull her hair out. However, on one occasion she went to her parents' home at about 11.00 pm, but neither of her parents or any of the children were there. She had subsequently found the children walking the streets nearby, so she took them home and put them to bed. It was after midnight before her mother returned home, and although not drunk – a state in which she had seen her on many occasions – she appeared to have been drinking.

Lastly, it was Mr Smart's turn to give evidence. He explained how on 12 August he returned home at about 2.15 pm to find his wife well on her way to being drunk or, as he described it, being 'about three parts on'. Instead of going out, he went to bed to wait until his daughter came home to go and do the shopping. He denied his wife's claim that he had burned her hand with the iron, but he admitted putting her clothes outside in the street, saying that he had told her to take the clothes out but she had refused to do so, and that was why he did it. Standing in the dock, holding his cap in both hands, he explained how he had on one occasion seen one of his daughters standing outside a 'public house'. When he asked her where her mother was, she replied that she was inside. He went in to find her and when he did, he asked her to come outside but she refused, saying that she would stay as long as she liked.

He was asked about the pawn tickets and he explained how he had found dozens of them in the home relating to items of clothing and footwear that belonged to him and the children, and none of the money his wife received went on buying any food. Her conduct had continually worsened over the years, which had resulted in him having to move the family on several occasions because their landlords were not prepared to put up with his wife's 'ill conduct'.

Having listened to all the evidence in the matter, the bench dismissed the case, but Mrs Smart's reaction to that decision was not recorded. It is interesting to think that while a matter such as this was being heard in a court in Poole and that the case was dismissed, it begs the question as to whether this was an incident that had actually taken place. If it had, any right-minded person would expect the full weight of the law to be laid across Smart's shoulders. If it was a false allegation made purely in an attempt to illicit monies from Smart, then it was equally disgusting but for different reasons. Yet while this court case was going on, men from Poole were away fighting in the war, doing their duty while trying their hardest to stay alive so that they could get back home to their loved ones.

In September 1917, the story of a wounded soldier came to light that was as remarkable as it could possibly be. The man in question was Harold Dredge, a private serving with the Hampshire Infantry Brigade, and who before the war was living with his parents, Mr and Mrs Dredge, at 'Jesmond Dene', Kingston Road, Longfleet, Dorset.

As far as most of us are concerned there is being lucky, there is being really lucky, and on the odd occasion there is the downright miraculous. This story comes from the latter category. Harold Dredge was involved in what was known as 'the great attack on July 31'. This apparently refers to the Third Battle of Ypres, specifically the very first day of the battle. During the fighting Harold was wounded, but not by a gunshot wound to an arm, leg, foot or hand. He was shot in the head by a bullet that entered at the front of his left ear and exited underneath his right eye, and he survived.

In October 1917, news was received that two brothers from Poole had both been wounded – Private Walter Palmer of Wimborne Road and Private Eric Palmer of Fernside Road – in the same battle. One was wounded in the neck, while the other was wounded in the shoulder. The 1911 census shows a Fred

Eric Palmer who was 31 years of age and working as a butcher, living with his parents, William and Mary Palmer, at Stanley Villa, Fernside Road, Longfleet. Checking back to the 1901 census shows there was a younger brother, Walter C. Palmer. There were also three other older brothers: William, Harry and Frank Palmer.

On Saturday, 13 October an inquest took place in front of the borough coroner, Mr E.J. Conway, at the Cornelia Hospital, Poole, in relation to the death of Arthur Kelley, a seaman. He was a married man who had lived with his wife Charlotte Louisa Kelley at 3 Mount Street, Poole. His wife had last seen him alive on the morning of Monday, 8 October, at which time he was in perfect health.

David Spanier, the master of a dredger, told the inquest that he owned a small motor launch that was on the foredeck of the vessel, having been taken on board at Newhaven. When they arrived back at Poole Harbour, they were in the process of transferring the launch from the dredger to the wharf when the stern of the boat struck Kelley on the shoulder, knocking him over. Mr Spanier was working the capstan and could not see clear to the boat, the deck of which was about level with the quay. He heard Kelley call out, 'Oh, come quick!' to which he responded by rushing round the quay where he found Kelley underneath the keel plate. He quickly had the motor launch lifted and had the ship's cook apply first aid, while a messenger was sent to call upon Doctor Malcolm Lamb.

Doctor Lamb told the inquest that when he arrived at the quayside, he found Kelley lying on the ground and noted the efficiency of the first aid that the injured man had been given. Apart from any internal injuries, the only obvious sign of injury he could see was a reasonably large, deep cut to the man's upper right thigh. Doctor Lamb called for an ambulance and had Kelley taken to the town's Cornelia Hospital. By the time he arrived at the hospital he was in shock due to serious blood loss. Although everything possible was done, Kelley never regained consciousness and died just after midnight on the Saturday morning. Death was due to the extensive blood loss and subsequent shock.

There was a question as to whether Kelley suffered from a mild form of deafness, although it was accepted that he was able to converse quite well in normal circumstances and it was not believed that this ailment in any way contributed to the accident. It was believed to have been exactly that: a complete and unfortunate accident.

Sunday, 18 November saw the time-honoured custom of 'Mayor's Sunday' observed on what was the second Sunday following the election of the town's new mayor, Major G.A. Dolby, who took over from Councillor Kentish, who became the deputy mayor. The new mayor attended the parish church of St James. As was usual on such occasions, there was an extremely large number of people in attendance, with the church 'packed to the rafters'. Before the church service, there was a lengthy procession from the Guildhall including members of the Corporation, borough officials and members of other public bodies including the military, the Fire Brigade, Superintendent William Bowles from the police, Captain S. Archer Phillips of the Poole Company, Dorset Volunteer Regiment, and Sergeant William Hitching who was in charge of a number of wounded soldiers. There were men from the Royal Naval Reserve and the local Naval Base in attendance, as were a large number of Sea and Land Scouts, under Scout Master Lavender. Other bodies and organizations represented included the King's Royal Rifle Cadets, the Poole Town Band, and the Poole Company, along with the Scouts' bugle bands.

The Reverend Reginald Fawkes was the man at the lectern delivering the sermon, with his remarks based on the letter sent by Paul to the church at Corinth. He said that the war was, as they all knew, still in the balance. What 'the civilization of our land would be in the future' depended largely on the generation that was involved in fighting the war. An enormous responsibility rested upon their shoulders, and they had to ensure that no matter what the cost, their inheritance of freedom was stoutly defended. As the reverend saw it, those at home could still play a massive part in the war effort, either in administration, legislation, the voluntary sector or individual influence over issues such as the environment or health.

Over Saturday and Sunday, 1 and 2 December, another pleasant weekend was enjoyed by several soldiers at the Poole Soldiers Home, which culminated with a Sunday social evening event, the festivities of which began at 8.15 pm. By way of a warm-up for the main evening's entertainment, Mr Benboe from London played a selection of pieces on the piano from 8.00 pm.

As the evening got under way, it was announced that Poole had lost another of its brave young men in the form of Lance Corporal 200738 (2402) Arthur Jesse Gritten, who was 24 years of age and the only son of Mr Jesse and Mrs Emily Gritten of 2 Maple Road, Poole. He had served with the 1st/4th Battalion, Dorsetshire Regiment, and prior to enlisting in the regulars, he had served in the Territorial Force for more than six years.

At the outbreak of war he had volunteered for active service and was then sent out to serve in India, leaving England on 2 September 1914. He remained in India for one year before then moving to Mesopotamia, where he saw active service. After having been away from home for nearly three years he was granted a period of six weeks' leave, but rather than return to England, he spent his well-deserved time off back in India, before once again returning to Baghdad and his colleagues. Soon afterwards he took part in the great advance, which led to so many Turkish soldiers being taken prisoner. It was during this time that he was killed in action on 28 October 1917. His body was found by a friend and colleague of his, Private Robert Old, who buried him as best he could. The Commonwealth War Graves Commission website records Arthur's death as being on Friday, 28 September 1917 and not October. He is buried at the Baghdad (North Gate) War Cemetery in Iraq.

In the British Army Service Records for those who served during the course of the Great War, there appears a Private 5720884 Robert Charles Old of 4 Emerson Road, Poole, Dorset, who when he enlisted in the regular army on 26 September 1914 at Dorchester was already 41 years of age. He was a member of the 1st/4th Battalion, Dorsetshire Regiment and had previously served with them as a Territorial soldier. Having said that, there is no absolute certainty that this is the same Robert Old who buried Arthur Gritten.

The person making the announcement about Gritten added that he knew they would all wish to offer their sympathies to the dead man's parents and sisters – Agnes, Lydia, Mabel and Eveline – as they undoubtedly struggled to come to terms with their sad loss.

As 1917 drew to a close, nobody would have known that this would be the last Christmas and New Year before the fighting and killing finally came to an end. By then everybody was tired and wanted an end to the conflict, but before that happened another ten and a half months would pass and during that period of time, British forces would lose another 209,682 men killed trying to bring the war to an end. Yet even that wouldn't be the end of it, as between 12 November 1918 and 31 December 1921, 49,278 more British soldiers would die of their wounds, illness or disease.

CHAPTER FIVE

1918: The Final Push

As 1917 became 1918, there were not many who would have guessed that year would be the first time in five years that people would be able to truly celebrate Christmas, although for the many who had lost loved ones to the war, even with the Armistice signed and the fighting at an end, it would still be a painful time.

The effects of the war on the people of Poole were not only felt in an emotional sense, but on people's stomachs as they were

DEFENCE OF THE REALM. E.P. 6.

MINISTRY OF FOOD.

BREACHES OF THE RATIONING ORDER

The undermentioned convictions have been recently obtained:—

Court	Date	Nature of Offence	Result
HENDON - -	29th Aug., 1918	Unlawfully obtaining and using ration books -	3 Months' Imprisonment
WEST HAM -	29th Aug., 1918	Being a retailer & failing to detach proper number of coupons	Fined £20
SMETHWICK -	22nd July, 1918	Obtaining meat in excess quantities - - -	Fined £50 & £5 5s. costs
OLD STREET -	4th Sept., 1918	Being a retailer selling to unregistered customer	Fined £72 & £5 5s. costs
OLD STREET -	4th Sept., 1918	Not detaching sufficient coupons for meat sold -	Fined £25 & £2 2s. costs
CHESTER-LE-STREET	4th Sept., 1918	Being a retailer returning number of registered customers in excess of counterfoils deposited - - - -	Fined £50 & £3 3s. costs
HIGH WYCOMBE	7th Sept., 1918	Making false statement on application for and using Ration Books unlawfully - - - - - - - -	Fined £40 & £6 4s. costs

Enforcement Branch, Local Authorities Division,
MINISTRY OF FOOD.
September, 1918.

Rationing fines leaflet.

now feeling the full force of the restrictions that the government had reluctantly placed on an individual's food intake.

Although there had been earlier restrictions on people's eating habits during the course of the war, the government had made a big issue out of its policy of 'business as usual', so it had been reluctant to impose any central control over the food markets, mainly because of their fears of how such a move would affect public morale. The government had steadfastly refused to impose minimum prices in relation to such food items as cereal production. In 1916 it became illegal to consume more than two food courses while out lunching in a public restaurant, or to eat more than three courses for dinner in the family home. It was even illegal to feed pigeons or stray animals, such as dogs.

Germany's policy of unrestricted submarine warfare in January 1917 was nothing more than a blatant attempt to try to starve Britain into surrendering. It was certain that something would have to be done in relation to the supply of all types of foodstuffs. This began with the idea of voluntary rationing by the public, which was introduced in February 1917. Bread was first subsidized in September 1917, and things were always going to get worse before they got better. By February 1918 Britain's wheat supplies were so low there was only six weeks' supply left. The situation culminated in ration books being introduced on 23 May 1918, restricting the food intake of each individual for such items as butter, margarine, lard, meat and sugar.

January 1918 saw the wartime death of Mr George Curtis at the age of 95. He had seen many changes in his illustrious lifetime, having been born just eight years after the Battle of Waterloo. His life connected the Georgian period to the Victorian era and beyond to the Great War. He had employed the time of his many years to good and useful public service, which saw him held in high esteem, affection and respect by all those who knew him. It wasn't just his age that drew people to him, it was what he did as a human being that endeared him to people.

When he started out on his journey through life, there were no railways, no steamboats, no penny post, no telegrams or telephones. Street lights and those that could be found in homes were meagre to say the least, and public roads were in a deplorable condition, hardly more advanced than dirt tracks, which with heavy rain made them almost unusable. Many commonplace facilities that were available in the early 1900s had not been so plentiful in his younger years when he was growing up. Battleships of the Royal Navy were nothing more complicated than large sailing vessels, and soldiers were armed with muskets that could only fire their projectiles a relatively short distance. Vice Admiral Horatio Nelson sailed to Trafalgar with a fleet of ships that a modern destroyer would have dealt with in less than an hour. The Duke of Wellington won the Battle of Waterloo with an army that a dozen machine guns could have wiped out in less than an hour. It took months to cross the world's oceans in sailing ships that relied heavily on a fair breeze to see them reach their destinations. Food and everyday living were comparatively simple in 1823, with none of the luxuries available to most towards the latter years of George's life.

Yet he didn't acquire the affectionate appellation of the 'Grand Old Man of Poole' merely because he was 94 years of age. Far from it, in fact. He took a deep and earnest interest in many aspects of life that made for the advancement of the human race in general and for the town of Poole as well.

For more than fifty years he held a seat on the town council. He had been an alderman and on four occasions he had also held the top civic post as the mayor of Poole. Anything that could be done to improve the conditions of life for the town's poor had his deep, if not sometimes cautious support. He wasn't just an ornamental figure on the council, but worked hard and zealously, and gave of his experience to those of his colleagues that he could help.

George began his working life as a builder before establishing a leading local business as an auctioneer and valuer. He was a founder of the Benefit Building Society. He was involved in educational matters and Poor Law work, and was a member of the board of guardians for more than fifty years. He had also been a magistrate without fear, favour or ill-will towards anybody. He was, as were most people of the time, a religious individual and a devoted follower of the Wesleyan Methodist church. He certainly earned the respect that people had for him and rightfully merited the title of 'the Grand Old Man of Poole'.

At the Poole Police Court, sitting before the mayor and other magistrates on Thursday, 14 February, Mrs May Cope of Salisbury Street, Poole was charged with permitting her premises to be used as a brothel, to which she pleaded not guilty. Police Sergeant Mills told the court that when he asked Mrs Cope to account for two men and two girls being in her house, she said that the soldier was related to her and his name was Wilson. Police Sergeant Mills subsequently found out that what he had been told wasn't correct.

Mrs Cope told the court that the other man, a sailor, had been having food at her home because there were no rations aboard his ship until 11.00 pm every day. The soldier tuned out to be a friend of her husband's at Portsmouth, where they had both been staying in the same barracks. She was found guilty as charged and sentenced to three months' imprisonment with hard labour. She was then charged with having neglected her children: Harry, who was just 21 months old, and daughter Nellie, who was just 6 months old. Once again, she pleaded not guilty to the charge.

Mr H. Tattersall was prosecuting this particular charge on behalf of the National Society for the Prevention of Cruelty to Children. His first witness was Police Inspector Edward Luff, who told the court that Mrs Cope was the wife of a driver in the Royal Engineers and received a weekly separation allowance of 24s 6d. The rent for the house was 5s a week. Although he found nothing physically wrong with the children when he visited, Inspector Luff said the baby was in a tin trunk that was resting on an old tea chest in the corner of the room, surrounded by rubbish and filth and covered with rags. In the bedroom, the room in the house where Mrs Cope, her two children and another woman slept, he could only describe the bed as a filthy mattress with no bedclothes on it.

The 6-month-old baby was dirty and thin, her breastbones and ribs clearly visible through emaciated skin. She was also suffering from a skin rash and bronchitis. There were sores on her bottom and legs where she had been sitting in her own excrement in the tin box. Inspector Luff explained to the court how he removed the baby from the house and took her to the workhouse infirmary on a magistrate's order; just in time, he believed, to save her life.

Dr Malcolm Lamb gave evidence that the child was suffering from acute bronchitis and although recently washed by the time he carried out his examination, she smelled offensively, he believed due to neglect. He described the child as being thin and wasting away, and in all probability, had she been allowed to remain in the house in the tin box under the conditions in which the house was found, she would have died. Despite the overwhelming evidence to the contrary, Mrs Cope claimed that she had not neglected her children. She was found guilty as charged and sentenced to four months' imprisonment with hard labour, to run concurrently with her other sentence.

Tuesday, 26 March saw the funeral of 9-year-old Jessie Phillips, the daughter of Mr and Mrs W.R. Phillips of North Road, Parkstone, take place at Poole cemetery. The child's father was a discharged soldier of the 8th (Postmen's) Battalion, City of London Rifles and was back in his old job as a postman at Parkstone. His daughter's coffin was borne by four members of the Royal Engineers from Wareham: Privates V. Morgan, J. Withers, Ken Le Vine and Cyril Harris. Numerous floral tributes had been laid at the graveside, including one from 'The Boys in Khaki', from her friends and teachers at St Peter's Girls School at Parkstone, and one from the superintendent junior teachers of the primary department of the Skinner Street Sunday School. It is believed the child died as a result of illness.

On the evening of Friday, 26 April there was a full meeting of the Poole War Memorial Committee which was held in the mayor's parlour at the Poole Guildhall. The sheriff, Councillor H. Ayre, was elected chairman for the meeting. A resolution was passed to the effect that 'All the ministers of all denominations in the Borough be co-opted', and a further resolution was also carried that 'all the public bodies, societies, clubs, and social organisations, throughout the borough, will be invited to send a representative from their organisation, and to elect a deputy to attend in the place of the main representative, if they are unable to attend for whatever reason.' The next meeting was to be held on Empire Day, 24 May 1918.

It was nice to see that in Poole they were ahead of the game when it came to their war memorial. They had decided to begin their arrangements while the war was still going on, unlike most towns and villages across the country that waited until after the war had ended before looking into commissioning such a memorial for erection in their own community.

In May 1918 news was received that Walter William Lugg, a bombardier in the Royal Field Artillery, had been wounded in action in the right leg during fighting in France, had subsequently been returned home to England and sent for treatment at the Keighley War Hospital, which included annexes at Morton Banks, Victoria Hospital, Fell Lane Infirmary, Spencer Street and Skipton in Yorkshire. While Walter was in hospital, the major general commanding his division wrote to him: 'I have read with great pleasure the report of your Regimental Commander and Brigade Commander regarding your gallant conduct and devotion to duty in the field on March 21st 1918.'

The 1911 census shows Walter living at 'Tivoli', Parkstone Road, Poole with his mother Annie Lugg, his sisters Flora, Mabel, Alice, Vera and Evelyn, and his brothers Charles and Reginald. He also had another brother, Arthur Louis Lugg, who served in the Royal Naval Reserve Service during the Great War, and during the Second World War served in the Merchant Navy. His father Charles Lugg died sometime between 1901 and 1911.

His brother Charles Ralph Lugg served as a Private (4544) in the 3rd/1st Battalion, Bucks Light Infantry, having enlisted at Poole on 20 January 1916. He was mobilized on 6 March 1916 and on 16 August 1916, he was medically discharged from the army for being a 'recruit with more than 3 months' service, considered medically unfit for further military service para 392 (iii)(cc) Kings Regulations.' He had served for just 164 days. Somehow, when he enlisted, the fact that one of his feet was deformed was missed at his medical. William also survived the war and lived until he was 90 years of age.

Mrs Brien of St Margaret's Road, Poole heard that her son, Sapper 249632 H.S. Brien, had been killed in action on 20 April while serving in Belgium with the Royal Garrison Artillery, to whom he was attached from the Royal Engineers. He had first arrived in France in October 1916. His commanding officer wrote the following letter to Sapper Brien's mother:

> I deeply regret to be the bearer of sad news with regard to Sapper H.S. Brien of my section. He was unfortunately killed in action late on the night of the 20th by a shell. He was badly hit in the thigh, arm and chest. He was buried at the farm at dawn on the Sunday morning by his colonel and comrades, a neat red cross erected and everything decently and reverently carried through. We parted with him with a deep sense of personal loss, for his gentlemanly bearing and quiet manners had endeared him to all of us. I personally feel that I have lost the best lad from the section.

After some anxious weeks of not knowing what had happened to their eldest son and whether he was dead or alive, Mr and Mrs T. Miles of the High Street, Poole discovered that he had been wounded and taken prisoner by the Germans. Lance Corporal T.I. Miles had been serving as a lance corporal with the Somerset Light Infantry during the heavy fighting at Saint-Quentin when he sustained a gunshot wound to his right foot.

The welcome news arrived in the form of a letter, sent from their son, who was in hospital at Limburg, Germany: 'A doctor dressed my wounds in the field, for which I am thankful.' He added that since he had been in hospital he had been treated very well and 'the sisters and nurses work hard and long to do all they can for us.' On the same ward as Lance Corporal Miles were five other Englishmen, six Frenchmen and five Italians. The other English patients, who had arrived at the hospital before Lance Corporal Miles, told him he was lucky becoming a patient at Limburg as they were looked after really well, and certainly better than they could ever have expected. He had been given his first shave since he had been taken prisoner when he arrived at the hospital by a wounded French soldier.

Mr and Mrs Miles' other son, E.L. Miles, was a private in the Cavalry Machine-Gun Corps, who had been serving in Egypt as part of the Egyptian Expeditionary Force. He had also been in hospital, not as a prisoner of war but because he had been suffering from diphtheria. On recovering, he was released from hospital to rejoin his battalion only to contract the same ailment for a second time, which saw him once again return to hospital.

On Saturday, 22 June 'Tank Week' came to an end in Poole, with the tank, which had been under the command of Lieutenant G. Hill, having been in place opposite the Gas Company's offices in the High Street. Having raised £117,000, it is fair to say that it was an extremely successful week for the tank's visit to Poole. Mayor G.A. Dolby was glowing in his praise of both the combined efforts of all those in the borough who had helped raise such a sum of money, and the Executive Committee of the Poole Central War Savings Committee who had organized and advertised the campaign so that as many people as possible were aware of the tank's presence in the town. The monies raised had surpassed the target sum of £100,000 set by the National War Savings Committee and by achieving this, Poole was now entitled to have an aeroplane bearing the town's name.

The idea behind Tank Week was to raise money for the war effort by helping to sell War Bonds and War Saving Certificates. Tanks were something totally new in warfare, and after their use at the Battle of Cambrai, which took place between 20 November and 6 December 1917, they quickly became a fascination for members of the general public. On 26 November 1917, a battle-scarred British tank, number 141, also affectionately known as 'Egbert', was put on display in Trafalgar Square after somebody on the National War Savings Committee decided to capitalize on the tank's appeal. It was an instant success; so much so that the campaign was extended to the entire country in an effort to maximize the amount of money raised. It was decided that the town or city that raised most money per capita head of population would win Egbert. It was won by the town of West Hartlepool, and first went on display there on 29 April 1919 where it remained until 1937 when it was scrapped by the West Hartlepool Town Council by 20 votes to 12 as it was deemed to be a 'relic of barbarism'. Yet just two years later, and with an element of irony, the Second World War began.

Mayor of Poole Mr G.A. Dolby wrote a letter in relation to the opening of the Borough of Poole United (Navy and Army) Service Club, which appeared in the *Bournemouth Guardian* on Saturday, 20 July. The purpose of the club was to provide a place for recreation and refreshment for the town's servicemen. The premises that had been secured for the club were situated in the High Street, opposite the Post Office. The work at the club was carried out under the auspices of the YMCA and in keeping with their ethos in relation to social and religious efforts.

The reason for the mayor's letter was to try to raise the estimated £150 needed for the club's necessary furniture and fittings. In addition, he was also asking for gifts of bagatelle boards, billiard tables, a piano, song music, games such as chess and draughts, and a regular supply of daily newspapers and magazines. Crockery and cooking utensils were required for the club's catering needs. Those wishing to make financial payments were asked to do so via Lloyds Bank in the High Street, and those who wished to donate gifts were asked to drop them in at the new premises after the following Wednesday.

On the evening of Wednesday, 7 August a recruiting meeting and rally took place in Poole Park. The mayor presided over the meeting, and representatives from both the military and Queen Mary's Army Auxiliary Corps were also in attendance. Proceedings began with a procession, starting from Poole railway station at 6.00 pm and marching through the town via Market Street, the Quay and High Street and on to the park, where the meeting began at 7.00 pm. A military band led the procession, with the women of the Queen Mary's Army Auxiliary Corps following them.

Mayor G.A. Dolby expressed his gratification at the large turnout, and added that he believed every fit woman should enrol in the corps, because in doing so she replaced a fit man who could then be released to go and serve in the army, directly helping the war effort. He recognized the hard work that women had been undertaking since the beginning of the war in all different spheres of work and volunteering. Yet there was more that needed to be done, and he hoped there would be a cordial response to the appeal for recruits to Queen Mary's Army Auxiliary Corps.

Colonel Harris, who was the commanding officer of the depot at Dorchester, said that part of his work was to encourage women between the ages of 18 and 50 to join the Women's Army. His job since 4 August 1914 had been to raise recruits for the men's army, at which he had been more than sufficient, and he was now hoping that he could offer that same level of experience to encouraging women to join up. He said that some 14,000 women were urgently required across the country, and hoped that the women of Poole would do their bit to contribute towards that figure. They were looking for women who were at the present time not doing anything of national importance, although married women with children were not high on their list. They were more concerned with young girls and single women. He received an update county by county of the number of women who had enlisted and sadly, he had to say that the county of Dorset was not presently high up on that list, but he hoped that it would not be long before that was at the top of the list.

Wednesday, 25 September saw the tragic death of 29-year-old Joseph Gaskell, a Private (T/438099) with the Reserve Supply Personnel Depot of the Army Service Corps. He was a married man, who before enlisting had lived with his wife Gertrude Gaskell of 78 Luther Street, Everton, Liverpool. He was buried at the Anfield cemetery in Liverpool.

At the time of his death, he was working with a group of his colleagues on the extension of the railway line at Sterte, tipping ballast, when a box broke, causing the cart to tip, and Gaskell was buried underneath it, sustaining very bad crush injuries, and died soon after he was admitted to the Cornelia Hospital in Poole. At the inquest, on the day after his death, a verdict of accidental death was returned by the jury.

In October 1918, information was received about a number of Poole men who were away fighting in the war. Mr Arthur H. Gooby, the youngest son of Mrs Emma Gooby of Holmwood, Sterte, Poole was serving as a Private (18907) with the 1st Battalion, Dorsetshire Regiment, and had been wounded for the third time. On the last occasion, he sustained gunshot wounds to both legs.

Lance Corporal and Chief Gunner 308078 Arthur Henry Lee, who was only 19 years of age, of 6 West Butts Street, Poole was serving with the 16th Battalion, Tank Corps at the time of his death. He had previously served with the Manchester Regiment, the Scottish Rifles and the Royal Scots. While serving with the Royal Scots, he suffered with rheumatic fever and septic poisoning. Having recovered from his illness, he had only been back in France for three weeks when he was killed in action on Sunday, 29 September. He was buried at the Unicorn Cemetery, Vendhuile, in the Aisne region of France.

He was a married man, his wife Sarah E. Lee, having moved to Manchester after the war. Second Lieutenant R.S. Andrews wrote a brief letter to Sarah after he was killed: 'He was always one of the cheeriest of my crew and as my chief gunner, was excellent. You will find comfort in the knowledge that your husband is now in God's keeping.' His mother Mrs Lee lived at Municipal Buildings, Ashley Cross, Lower Parkstone.

Gunner A.R. Sartin was serving with a siege battery when he was severely wounded in the left thigh. Initially he was admitted to the general hospital in Wimereux, France, but was later sent back to England and admitted to the Ontario Military Hospital in Orpington, Kent. His home was at Denmark Road, Poole.

Harry Pearce was 32 years of age and died of his wounds sustained while fighting in France and is buried there at the Fortequenne Cemetery. In 'Civvy Street', back home in England, he was by profession a tailor.

Private 230383 Gilbert Saunders of the Cavalry of Horse was wounded in action on 27 September. His father, Albert

Herbert Saunders, was informed by the Cavalry Record Office that his son had been wounded. He had served in Egypt from 22 April 1915 as part of the Egyptian Expeditionary Force. He had previously served with the Dorset Yeomanry as a Private (920). 'Gilby' Saunders, the name by which he was affectionately known, was, before he enlisted in the army, one of the most active members of the Poole Amateur Rowing Club and well-liked by all who knew him. Work-wise he was a hawker, selling floor cloths, baskets and chairs.

The 1911 census showed that Gilbert lived at Beresford Road, Upper Parkstone, Dorset with his parents, William and Mary Saunders, his six sisters, Liberty, Mary, Nellie, May, Violet and Ivy together with brother Albert. He was discharged from the army on 22 February 1919 as no longer physically fit for military service.

On the evening of Monday, 4 November, just one week from the end of the war, an important and interesting lecture took place at the Unitarian Schoolroom. The lecture by Mr George Castle from Parkstone was on the subject of Poole and its possibilities of national development and usefulness in respect of harbour, port and district.

Mr Castle was connected to the works that were carried out on the east side of the harbour in that he was an advisor to the government and private companies in respect of the capabilities of the southern ports for mercantile developments. He began by saying that his impression was that Poole might have made far more of itself than it had done, especially as it had great natural advantages. He said that he would only recommend what was beneficial for a town and port that was so centrally situated; nothing would be allowed to mar the beauty of the neighbourhood.

There was the cross-Channel traffic for both passenger and cargo vessels, which had previously been mainly run out of Southampton. That had become a tad congested, because as the port was able to take larger vessels, they had become somewhat impeded by smaller ones. The advantage of Poole in terms of which town might be selected to take some of the traffic from Southampton was that Poole to France would be 30 miles nearer than it was from Southampton, and rail travel to the West Country and the Midlands region was easier to reach from Poole than it was from Southampton.

The lecture also ventured into the area of ship-building as well as for yachts, which in the latter case also included design and repair. Mr Castle finished his talk by commenting on the town itself. Something needed to be said about the general improvements required to the town. The streets, he said, were too narrow and tortuous and needed replacing. He had no desire to knock the heart and soul out of the town; in fact he intended to keep and preserve 'what was old and picturesque, but retention of the old, ugly and insanitary was surely a mistake.' It could be done, he said, without any loss to an enterprising borough, and he suggested that the values created would far outweigh those that were destroyed in the process.

Mr Castle's lecture caused, as one might imagine, some lively and animated discussion. At the end of the evening there were strong objections to the proposals for the new High Street and the yacht club house, but overall many of those in attendance agreed with his suggestions.

On Monday, 25 November a meeting of the Poole Rural District Council took place. There were many points of discussion, including food control, a proposed conference for Rural District Council Associations, the 'flu epidemic and the relaxation of building bye-laws. The latter of these topics caused particular widespread discussion in relation to accommodation for working-class people. Now that the Armistice had been signed, the general feeling among the masses was a desire to move forward to a better tomorrow and to ensure that the pain, suffering and sacrifice that had occurred during the war years were not all in vain.

Housing accommodation in the area of Poole was generally regarded as entirely inadequate. Added to this, the sanitation standards and water supply throughout Poole and its surrounding districts were considered to be very defective. It was considered essential that any increase in housing accommodation should take into account the highlighted issues of sanitation and water supply. By way of providing perspective and balance to the discussion, it was pointed out that the water supply in the rural district was very satisfactory, that there was a sewage scheme being considered for Broadstone, and everything was regarded as being quite satisfactory. There was no actual detail attached to those final comments, so what that actually meant in real terms is unclear. What was clear from the meetings of the Poole Rural District Council that followed the signing of the Armistice was a positivity and a desire to move forward in all areas of life for the benefit of everybody. Whether mentioned or just subliminal, it was clear to see that people wanted a better tomorrow in all areas of their lives. Returning to how things had been before the war was simply not a realistic proposition.

By the time the war was over, many families across the country had paid a terrible price for their nation's victory. There were many examples of families sending more than one of their loved ones to fight in the hope of a final victory and a better tomorrow, and the town of Poole was no exception.

The 1911 census included details of the Maidment family who lived at 1 Heath View Terrace, Davis Road, Upper Parkstone. Parkstone, an area of Poole, is split into the two areas of Upper and Lower Parkstone for obvious geographical reasons, with Upper Parkstone sitting as it does on higher ground, while Lower Parkstone sits more towards Poole Harbour.

Walter Charles Maidment was born in Yeovil, Somerset in 1855. In the spring of 1879 Walter, by then 24 years of age, married Susan Jane Barter, aged 25, in Walter's home town, where they initially set up home at 46 Sparrow Lane Cottages. Walter earned his living as a painter, and their first child, Anne, was born the following year.

However, the 1891 census caused some confusion. Although the same Walter Maidment appears, his place of birth and occupation were the same and his age of 36 was as it should have been, the family had not only moved address, they had moved to a different town in another county, which found them living at 194 Lime Kiln Road, Bourne Valley, Kinson, Dorset.

For some reason Walter's wife Susan had become Lucy, but she was the same age as Susan would have been, 37, and was born in the same town of Beaminster, Dorset. Daughter Annie was by then 10 years of age, which was right, and the family had increased in size with the addition of four more children: Frederick, aged 9; George, aged 5; Harry, aged 6; and Walter, aged 3. Susan was still alive as she didn't die until March 1945 at the age of 91 in Poole.

The next census didn't make things any clearer. The family home was now at 242 Leyton Road, Branksome, Dorset. Susan Jane Maidment, born in Beaminster, Dorset in 1854, was now back as Mrs Maidment, suggesting that the 1891 entry where her name had been recorded as Lucy was nothing more than a mistake by the census-taker. Now her husband's name had changed to William C. Maidment, he was still a painter and ten years older, the age that Walter would have been, and he was born in Yeovil. Annie Maidment was now 20 years of age and living in Bournemouth as a servant with the Toerner family. Son Frederick was now 18 years of age, William was 15, Walter was 13, and Arthur was just 8. (Once again, any name changes or age discrepancies appear to be nothing more than clerical errors by those completing the census in question.)

On the outbreak of the Great War, a number of the Maidment sons enlisted and went off to fight. Frederick John, the oldest of the Maidment children, was a married man by the time he enlisted in the Royal Flying Corps (RFC) on 31 May 1917. It would appear from his service record, and despite the fact that he had been a master tailor in Civvy Street, he became an Airman, Second Class (F 29880). His last service date was 31 March 1918, despite the fact that he had signed on for the duration of hostilities. He survived the war.

George William Maidment was serving as a Private (17697) with the 6th Battalion, Dorsetshire Regiment when he died of wounds on 7 December 1916 at the 1st Australian General Hospital, Rouen, and was buried at the St Sever cemetery extension at Rouen in the Seine-Maritime region of France. He was 24 years of age.

Walter Charles Maidment enlisted in the army and became a Private (21036) in the 1st/6th Battalion, Royal Warwickshire Regiment, which was a Territorial unit. He was killed in action on 4 February 1917 while serving on the Western Front in France.

The War Diaries for the 1st/6th Battalion, Royal Warwickshire Regiment for 4 February 1917 show that the battalion was in trenches at Biaches and had been for two days. Biaches is a small village situated in the Somme region of France. In 2006 the entire population was still only 423 people. The battalion's War Diary entry for 4 February 1917 was as follows:

> Heavily bombarded between 12 (noon) and 5.40 pm, with three slight lulls. Intense bombardment 5.40 – barrage on Front. Support and STETTIN lines and Communication Trenches. Raiding parties entered left of centre company (B.Co) at 6.15 pm – Other parties on right and left stopped by LG and rifle fire. SOS signals sent up 6.15 and HQ communicated with Brigade on telephone, just as line were out, Centre and left companies moved up supports, found enemy already driven out at 6.25 pm. Casualties, 2/Lt. FJT Belcher killed – OR 34 killed. 4 died of wounds. 66 wounded. 14 missing. Opposed by 1st Prussian Guard.

Walter Charles Maidment was one of thirty-four members of the 6th Battalion, Royal Warwickshire Regiment killed in action on 4 February 1917. The battalion was relieved the following day, and sent back to the rear trenches and beyond for a break, some hot food, a shower and some much-needed sleep.

Arthur Edward Maidment was a Corporal (36152) in the 9th (Service) Battalion, Leicestershire Regiment when he was killed in action on Thursday, 22 November 1917 on the Western Front. When he had initially enlisted in the army he had served as a Private (20875) with the Devonshire Regiment. He was buried in the Communal Cemetery Extension at Hersin-Coupigny in the Pas-de-Calais region of France. A slight anomaly arises here, as despite the Commonwealth War Graves Commission website stating that he was buried in France, the Army's Register of Soldiers' Effects covering the period 1901–1929 states that he was killed in action in Belgium.

Walter and Susan Maidment certainly paid a very high price for their family's involvement in the Great War with the death of their three sons George, Walter and Arthur.

Finally, the war was over. The Armistice was signed and the fighting came to an end at 11.00 am on 11 November 1918, but even on the final day 631 British soldiers were either killed or died of wounds, illness or disease.

The people of Poole had most definitely done their bit in keeping their nation free from the grip of an aggressive and determined enemy, one who had been hell-bent on enslaving the people of the United Kingdom. Fortunately it was not to be, and British resolve finally won the day.

CHAPTER SIX

1919: The Aftermath

The war was over at long last, but not all British soldiers returned home immediately; there were many who had to remain in Europe to deal with the aftermath of the conflict. There would be changes for everybody and nothing was ever going to be the same again. It never could be after everything that had taken place since 1914.

On a global scale, there had been a revolution in Russia in 1917 and there had also been a mutiny in the French army the same year. Four pre-war empires were no more: Austria-Hungary, Russia, Germany and the Ottoman Empire. New countries were born, rising like a phoenix from the ashes of what had been before, and the map of Europe changed dramatically as new borders sprang up all over the place. There had been a 'flu pandemic throughout 1918 (the so-called 'Spanish 'flu'), causing an estimated loss of life of some 50 million people. A sad irony was that the epicentre of the pandemic's beginnings was identified by the renowned virologist John Oxford of the Royal London Hospital and St Bartholomew's Hospital as occurring at the troop staging and hospital camp at Étaples, France.

Closer to home in Britain, unemployment had become a major issue. Women who had been employed during the war, mainly in jobs that were previously the sole domain of men, wanted to keep their new-found independence which had opened up a world to them outside of the home. Employers wanted to hang on to their female workers, mainly because they were paid less than a man to do the same job. However, the men who had left their jobs to serve their country when required now wanted to work and they wanted their old jobs back. Yet this wasn't just about who had jobs and who didn't; it was about natural, expected changes after the end of the war. Munitions factories were dramatically reduced in numbers, as were the factories producing aircraft, tanks and artillery pieces. Ship-building saw a sharp reduction in the number of vessels required, especially those for the Admiralty. Technology steadily improved, meaning that fewer people were needed for the same output, and for those who were employed, many found their working hours were reduced.

People's expectations of what they wanted from this new beginning were largely based on what they had been through during the war. For those with military service, many of them had killed enemy soldiers and seen their friends and colleagues killed all around them. They had done their duty, so to have a job of work to come home to didn't seem too much to expect in return. In this respect the men of Poole who had served and fought for their country were no different, and their expectations were exactly the same.

Even though the war was now over, its memories would linger in the mind for ever more. So the chance to meet up with a group of comrades who would have some idea of what their colleagues had experienced was too good to miss.

On Thursday, 1 May a supper and social evening took place at the Heckford Park Drill Hall, Bournemouth. The evening's events had been organized by officers and NCOs of the 1st (Poole) Company, Dorset Volunteer Regiment. The gathering was to celebrate the signing of the Armistice, and to recognize the good work carried out by the members of the regiment since it came into being on 16 October 1914. The drill hall was colourfully decorated, as might be expected to mark such a joyous occasion, and was the responsibility of Sergeant Vick, while the catering for the evening fell to a subcommittee consisting of Lieutenant Yeatman, Company Quarter Master Sergeant Grainger, Sergeants Dennis and Holloway and Lance Corporal S. Watkins.

The presiding officer for the evening's event was Captain S.A. Phillips, supported by the commanding officer of the 1st (Poole) Company, Dorset Volunteer Regiment, Colonel Kindersley-Porcher, whose son Captain Robert Erskine Kindersley died on 31 May 1945, three weeks and three days after the war had ended in Europe. He is buried at the Groesbeek Canadian War Cemetery in Holland, and had been serving with the Royal Canadian Engineers.

There was an excellent turnout with more than 150 men in attendance. After dinner a toast list and musical programme took place, starting with the loyal toast which resulted in everybody to a man rising and standing in silence in memory and out of respect to those of their comrades who had fallen in the war. In the toast given by Captain Phillips, he spoke of how the officers and instructors had been encouraged by HQ to use their own initiative as much as possible. As far as 'A' Company was concerned, they had been allowed to carry out their work to the best of their ability with little or no interference from those at HQ.

Colonel Kindersley-Porcher gave a speech about how he had begun his military service back in 1878, and since that time he had seen all sorts of conditions of troops, both in time of war and peace, but throughout all of his years of service he had never been more glad to serve than he was for the previous two years with the men of the Dorset Volunteers. He had found it hard to deal with being too old a 'buffer' not to be able to take his own battalion, which he raised, commanded and trained, out to France but those who had gone, he both honoured and greatly respected. In fact, he respected all men who had served, whether they had volunteered out of a sense of duty and honour or because they had been compelled to do so by conscription or the fear of being labelled a coward. He accepted, however, that some men were honestly prevented from enlisting in the armed forces because of genuine family or hardship reasons.

He mentioned the service that his company had performed by doing duty on the guard ship at the entrance to Poole Harbour in 1914, by supplying a coastal patrol of twenty to thirty officers and men from the Poole and Branksome detachment in 1915 and the following three years, and by furnishing the Hamworthy Magazine guard. The Poole Volunteers were the first to be formed in the county of Dorset, and they knew only too well how Captain Gotto had raised the company and worked from the start until he handed over the command to Captain Phillips, who had carried it on with the same devotion and efficiency. Since Captain Gotto had been appointed adjutant, he had been able to judge his efficiency and self-denying exertions.

Colonel Kindersley-Porcher proceeded to pay tribute to the work of all the officers of the company, as well as the non-commissioned officers and men. In his conclusion, he read a letter from General Sir Henry Sclater, GCB, Commander-in-Chief Southern Command, testifying to the excellent services of the volunteers, their admirable spirit, example of self-sacrifice and anxiety to render themselves efficient.

The colonel then presented to Lieutenant Leonard Sturdy, in commanding the Wareham detachment, a cup he had offered for the efficiency of detachments both in drill and attack movements. He congratulated the company on winning the cup and above all, the Wareham detachment. Out of a possible total of 100 marks Wareham had amassed 80 points; Gillingham had a score of 74; Dorchester 72; Weymouth 69; and Bridport 62. Captain Gotto submitted 'A' Company, referring to their excellent work. He also mentioned the large amount of time and energy that the colonel had devoted to the work of the battalion; words that he spoke out of genuine belief rather than any attempt at currying favour with the colonel.

As has been mentioned, it was an evening full of toasts that included 'Returning Service Men', 'The Visitors', 'The Officer Commanding', 'The Catering Committee' and last but not least, 'The Artisans'. It sounds like an evening involving much back-slapping and self-indulgent congratulations but with the war finally over, maybe these were justifiable platitudes.

In celebration of 1 May as Labour Day, the Poole Trades and Labour Council held a public meeting in the Liberal Hall, Wimborne Road on the evening of Thursday, 1 May. The meeting was well-attended, with Mr Harry Brookes, JP, presiding. He appealed to the trade unions to take action to find employment for the thousands of brave lads who had returned from the war and were now walking the streets. Even if they had to reduce the daily hours of work of those already in employment to just four, they were encouraged to do so if it would help find some work for all the men seeking employment.

Mr John Rees was a miners' agent from Neath in South Wales. He was present to provide a Welsh perspective and an example of how Welsh miners had been treated by some elements of the government for simply standing up for their rights, which many felt they had more than earned in blood, sweat and tears while fighting in the war. Mr Rees spoke of how Lloyd George had been successful in getting coal at the beginning of the war and also acquiring sufficient numbers of munitions as the Minister of Munitions; that being the case, he didn't understand that now the government was speaking of the nation needing 1 million new homes, what was stopping them appointing a Minister of Housing? This would create work for unemployed men. Mr Rees continued by stating that the nation's workforce had been 'gulled' at the last General Election. By that he meant members of parliament had been voted in who would never come up with the number of houses required. The subsequent shortfall would be their responsibility and not that of the working man. It was, he said, part of the government's attempts at keeping the working man 'down' and 'in his place'. There was no other logical explanation why the housing he spoke of, which was so urgently required, was not yet being built.

He appealed to those present at the meeting to join the Labour movement. The war had been hellish, of that there was no doubt. Men who had gone off to fight in the war when called to do so had done this without 'batting an eyelid' because it had been a matter of honour and duty to them. Now it was the turn of the government to do the right thing by them.

It was at this stage of the meeting that the chairman presented Mr W. Lloyd with a clock and a cheque for £32 0s 9d in recognition of his actions during the dock workers' strike at Poole quay in Poole Harbour in August 1918. The incident referred to was the refusal of Mr Lloyd, who was a member of a military party ordered to do the work of strikers, to work. For his stance, his point of principle, he was charged and put before the courts, and despite being defended and supported by Poole's Trades and Labour Council, Mr Lloyd was found guilty and sentenced to two years' imprisonment. The clock was purchased out of the money raised for his defence and the cheque was the residual sum.

The afternoon of Sunday, 19 October saw the final parade of 'A' Company, 1st Volunteer Battalion, Dorset Regiment at the Danecourt field. Representatives were also present from Poole, Branksome and Wareham detachments, all of whom were under the command of Captain S.A. Phillips. Other officers present were the adjutant Captain W. Gotto, Lieutenant N.G. Yeatman, Lieutenant H.J. Fellowes, Second Lieutenant L. Sturdy (Wareham) and Second Lieutenant D. Stewart (West Moors). There were also about 100 NCOs and men on parade wearing full uniform.

The adjutant, Captain W. Gotto, addressed the company, thanking them all for the service they had rendered to their community and their nation throughout the war years. The 1st Dorset Volunteers, he said, were considered by the Southern Command to be the best volunteer battalion in the entire command. They had done some very useful work, and he was sorry that the time had come for them to be disbanded. They were discharged from their duties as of 15 October 1919. Each and every man of the company was presented with a certificate of service by Captain Gotto.

The company had first been formed in November 1914 in the early months of the war, the original unit being known as the Athletes' Volunteer Corps. The first voluntary work that the company carried out was helping to guard Poole Harbour by providing both day and night patrols. These patrols were continued, around the clock, all the way through until the summer of 1918. In addition to these duties, 'A' Company also provided a guard for the Hamworthy Magazine for a period of more than eighteen months. At the end of the afternoon's proceedings, the company had its final photograph taken.

Of the 49,278 British servicemen who died between 12 November 1918 and 31 December 1921, the ten listed below were from Poole or had Poole connections:

Private 210861 Ernest Albert Foot of the 1st/4th Battalion, Hampshire Regiment died on 12 November 1918. His parents, George and Jane Foot, lived at 3 Kendall's Alley, Poole.

Private 27906 F.G. Blake of the 6th Battalion, Wiltshire Regiment died on 13 November 1918. His parents, George and Annie Blake, lived at 3 High Street, Poole.

Deck Hand 18798/DA Francesco Cicillo Bancone of the Royal Naval Reserve died on Wednesday, 19 February 1919. His father lived at 17 Shaftesbury Road, Poole.

Sergeant Major 252 David Martin, Military Medal, Meritorious Service Medal, Mentioned in Dispatches three times, RAF, died on Monday, 24 February 1919. His widow lived at 'Hollyhurst', Fernside Road, Poole.

Private 265590 Thomas Norman Haynes, 11th Battalion, Somerset Light Infantry, died on Saturday, 8 March 1919. His parents, William and Clara Haynes, lived at 'Ferndale', St Margaret's Road, Poole.

Driver T4/212127 Harry Butcher of the 800th Heavy Transport Company, Royal Army Service Corps, died on 12 May 1919. His wife, Lilian Bessie Butcher, lived at 75 Green Road, Poole.

Gunner 101455 A.C. Ayres of the 199th Siege Battery, Royal Garrison Artillery, died on 19 June 1919. His parents, Walter and Eliza Ayres, lived in Poole.

Sapper WR/209421 P.B.P. Penny of the ROTD, Royal Engineers, died on 24 June 1919. His parents, Thomas and Elizabeth Penny, lived at 23 Market Street, Poole.

Private 5926 Nicholas John Paice served with the Royal Defence Corps and died on 20 December 1919. He was born in Poole.

Private 27380 Albert Benjamin George Holloway of the Wiltshire Depot Regiment died on Wednesday, 19 May 1920. His parents, Charles and Sarah Holloway, lived at Creekmore, Poole.

CHAPTER SEVEN

Poole War Memorial

Poole War Memorial.

The Municipal War Memorial, erected in Poole Park, was unveiled and dedicated on 16 October 1927; somewhat unusual as many of the other memorials situated in towns and villages around the country were in place by 1921 and 1922. Poole did, in fact, have a war memorial to commemorate the names of the town's dead that had been unveiled at St Michael's Church in Hamworthy in July 1919, eight years prior to the town's Municipal War Memorial.

To the best of the author's ability, here are the names of the men and women of Poole who lost their lives as a result of their involvement in the Great War:

Adams, G.L.
Adey, Frederick Cecil
Alderson, Alex George James
Aldridge, James (1914)
Aldridge, Reginald (1915)
Aldridge, T.
Allen, Charles (1917)
Allen, Edwin (1915)
Allen, Fred
Allen, Frederick James (1914)
Allen, G.
Allen, John Robert (1914)
Allen, Mark (1917)
Allen, Sidney Charles (1914)
Allen, W.F. (1917)
Allen, William James (1918)
Anderson, A.M.
Anderson, E.D.
Anderson, T.B.
Andrews, Ernest George
   (1918)
Andrews, Harold Robert
   Victor (1917)
Angel, George (1916)
Angel, John (1915)

Angel, Percy (Harry) (1918)
Arnold, Arthur Edward
   (1918)
Ault, H.F.
Ayles, Stanley (1916)
Ayley, Alfred Henry (1919)
Ayley, Frederick Ernest
   (1918)
Ayley, John Alfred (1915)
Ayres, A.C.

Bacon, Douglas Haviland
   (1916)
Baker, Alfred Thomas
   (1915)
Baker, Fred Douglas (1916)
Baker, R.
Baker, Reginald (1917)
Baker, Walter Gilbert (1917)
Baldwin, John O. (1917)
Ball, Albert Thomas
   Augustus (1916)
Ballam, James John
Ballett, George (1918)
Balston, Harry Love (1915)

Bancone, Francesci Cicillo (1919)
Bargery, Sidney Walter (1916)
Barnes, J.E.
Barnes, James (1916)
Barnes, Sidney Joseph
Barnes, William (1917)
Bartlett, Joe
Bartlett, Joseph Thomas (1915)
Bartlett, William Albert
Barton, Reginald James (1917)
Bascombe, William Albert (1916)
Baverstock, Charles (1915)
Beament, Arthur Willie (1917)
Bean, M.G.
Beaumont, Thomas Somerville (1917)
Belben, Harry (1918)
Belcher, F.E.
Beckingham, James (1917)
Beckwith, Frederick Henry (1917)
Bennett, Jack
Bennett, Percy Frank (1916)
Bennett, Reginald Percy (1916)
Best, Frederick (1915)
Biggs, Alfred James Christian (1918)
Biles, Bertram William (1918)
Bishop, H.
Bishop, James Henry (1918)
Blake, A.

Blake, Edward Geoffrey (1916)
Blake, F.G. (1918)
Blake, Henry James (1916)
Blake, William Edward (1919)
Blandford, Edwin Clement Haskett (1916)
Bloomfield, Percy Leonard
Bogart, William Joseph Germain (1918)
Bowditch, William George (1918)
Bowering, John (1917)
Bowering, Robert John (1915)
Bowman, Samuel George Pascoe (1917)
Bowring, Henry Frank (1917)
Brackstone, Frank Wilfred (1916)
Brackstone, Frederick Arthur (1918)
Brackstone, Herbert (1919)
Brackstone, Herbert Chennet (1915)
Brackstone, Robert William (1918)
Bradford, Harry Alfred James (1917)
Bratcher, Frederick Arthur (1918)
Brazier, Albert Henry
Bridle, Ernest (1918)
Bridle, Ernest Charles (1919)
Brien, Harold Samuel (1918)
Briggs, Alfred James Christian
Brocklehurst, Evelyn Pierrepont (1918)

Bromby, Walter Thomas (1917)
Broomfield, DSM, G.
Brown, Arthur George (1915)
Brown, B.C.
Brown, Edward Ernest
Brown, Frank (1916)
Budden, B.
Budge, Hubert Lionel (1916)
Budge DSO, Philip Prideaux (1918)
Bugden, Ralph (1917)
Bungay, Frederick (1917)
Bungay, George (1915)
Bunter, William Frederick
Bungay, James (1919)
Burden, Albert Millian (1917)
Burden, William Samuel (1917)
Burles, Charles (1914)
Burrows, H.
Burn, Charles Scott (1917)
Butcher, Harry (1919)
Butler, Alfred John (1917)
Butler, Thomas William (1916)

Café, Thomas (1916)
Caplin, Joseph Harry (1917)
Carey, George (1917)
Carter, George (1917)
Carter, John Laws (1918)
Cartridge, Joseph George Edward (1917)
Cartridge, William John (1915)
Case, Montague Vaughan (1918)

Case, Walter Edward (1918)
Cave, Reginald George (1918)
Cave, Sidney Arthur (1916)
Cave, Walter James (1917)
Chaddock, Walter Edward Victor (1918)
Chaffey, William Thomas (1918)
Chalkley, Ernest (1917)
Chambers, A.
Cherrett, Alfred Thomas (1915)
Cherrett, Arthur William (1917)
Cherrett, Cyril Joseph Maurice (1917)
Chinchen, Frederick William (1916)
Christmas, R. Christopher
Christopher, Fredrick Bertie (1917)
Churchill, Seth (1917)
Clarke, Frederick George (1915)
Clarke, P.A.
Clayton, William (1916)
Clough, Hugh Francis (1917)
Cobb, Walter Edward (1918)
Cobb, Walter James (1916)
Cobb, Walter Sydney (1916)
Cobb, William John (1916)
Cobbett, C.N. (1919)
Cochrane, William Alexander (1916)
Colburne, Harold
Coles, Arthur G.
Coles, Cyril William (1916)

Coles, Melnoth William
  Alister (1917)
Coles, Richard Frederick
  (1917)
Coles, W.
Coombes, Edwin
Cooper, Douglas Eric John
  (1916)
Cooper, Edward Thomas
Cooper, John (1915)
Cooper, Henry
Cooper, William George
  Henry
Corbin, Arthur Elliott (1916)
Court, Leonard Augustus
  (1916)
Coward, Frederick James
  (1916)
Cox, Archibald Sidney John
Cox, F.
Cox, Harold Frank
Cox, Wilfred Arthur (1917)
Crabb, Alfred Leslie (1916)
Crabb, William Victor (1917)
Crane, Cecil (1916)
Critchell, Walter (1914)
Curtis, E.T.
Curtis, Frederick Walter (1916)
Curtis, J.C.
Cutler, Charles (1917)
Cutler, Charles Edwin (1917)
Cutler, Frederick William
  (1918)
Cutler, Walter (1919)

Damon, Albert Edward (1915)
Dandois, H.J.J.

Darley, Harry
Davis, James Richard (1916)
Day, Stewart Arbuthnot
  (1917)
De Lisle-Smith, Frank (1918)
Dean, Ernest Frederick
  (1916)
Dean, F.
Dean, R.J.
Dean, William Harold (1915)
Dennis, Percy Victor (1916)
Dent, Wilfred Brown (1918)
Derrick, Ernest J. (1918)
Dick, Arthur James Seaber
  (1918)
Diffey, William (1917)
Diment, Albert Victor (1916)
Diment, William Henry
  (1917)
Dix, Thomas (1914)
Dolman, Ernest (1919)
Dolman, Henry
Dolman, Sidney Albert (1918)
Dolman, Walter (1914)
Draper, Ernest Goulding
  (1916)
Draper, Horace Sydney (1916)
Drew, T.
Durant, Christopher Gilbert
  (1916)
Dyason, Reverdy Cecil (1918)
Dyer, Frederick George (1914)
Dyer, Percival Ernest (1914)
Dyett, Alfred George Charles
  (1918)
Dyett, Harry W. (1918)
Dyke, C.

Dyke, Walter Harry (1917)

Earney, George (1917)
Eastwood, William
Edwards, Leonard Neeson
Effemey, Leonard (1915)
Elliot, Alfred Reginald (1917)
Ellis, George Frederick
  William (1919)
Ennis, Alfred Ernest (1915)
Evans, W.
Eveley, Charles (1915)

Facey, William (1916)
Fair, William Henry (1918)
Fancey, Percy (1915)
Fancy, E. Farquharson
Fawell, Nathan (1918)
Featy, W.E.
Ferrett, W.J. (1919)
Fielder, George Ernest (1918)
Fish, Frederick John (1916)
Fisher, A.E.
Fisher, Albert Charles (1916)
Fisher, Ernest Edward (1917)
Fisher, H.S.
Fleet, Colin (1918)
Fletcher, James Henry (1917)
Foot, Ernest Albert (1918)
Foot, Thomas (1914)
Foot, W.J.
Fordham, W.G.
Foster, Arthur
Foster, Walter Arthur (1919)
Fowle, Charles Henry (1918)
Francis, Howard Walter
  (1918)

Francis, T.E.
Fray DCM, William
Freeborne, Henry (1916)
Freke, Edgar Charles (1917)
French, Robert George (1918)
Fresheny, Frank
Frizzel, Frederick George
  (1918)
Frost, DCM, Charles George
Froud, Arthur Charles (1918)
Froud, John Chubb (1918)
Fry, Leonard George (1916)
Fudge, Alfred Henry (1916)
Fudge, Edward John (1915)
Fudge, E.S.
Fuller, R.F.

Gale, Cecil James Best (1917)
Gale, William George (1917)
Gallop, Harry John (1919)
Garland, Albert Edward
  (1917)
Garland, Harold Joseph
  (1918)
Garrard, Frederick
Garrett, George
George, William Henry
Gibbs, Arthur (1916)
Gibbs, Bertie (1917)
Gibbs, Frank Benjamin (1915)
Gibbs, Frederick Henry (1916)
Gibbs, George (1918)
Gibbs, S.
Gibbs, Sidney Thomas (1916)
Gifford, Leslie Frank (1917)
Gilbert, Garnet
Gilbert, Valentine

Gilham, Reginald James (1918)
Gilham, William Charles
   (1918)
Gill, Valentine John Adey
   (1917)
Gillett, Walter John (1918)
Gillingham, Albert Ernest
   (1918)
Gillingham, Leonard (1918)
Gillingham, Percy Job (1918)
Gillingham, Victor William
   Henry (1918)
Gillingham, William James
   (1915)
Glasson, R.G.
Goff, Edgar Frederick (1915)
Gollop, Albert Edward (1915)
Goom, F.V.C.
Goom, J.F.
Goom, W.
Gould, Alfred George (1919)
Gould, Charles (1918)
Gould, Charles (1916)
Gould, John James (1915)
Grant, Charles Archibald
   (1916)
Gray, A.
Gray, William (1916)
Green, F.
Green, Percy
Greenslade, A.
Greenslade, Arthur Charles
   (1917)
Greenwood, Ralph
Grey, H.
Gribbell, Leslie Terrell
   Gillingham, Percy C.

Griffin, Stanley (1917)
Gritten, Arthur Jesse (1917)
Guest, J.S.
Guest, John Eric Cox
Gurney, William J. (1918)

Habgood, Albert James
Habgood, Percy Fred (1916)
Hale, James (1917)
Hales, Albert Alexander
   (1917)
Hall, William
Hampton, Edward Bertie
   (1915)
Handsford, E.
Hardy, Thomas Frank
   (1916)
Harker, J.
Harland, Tom George (1918)
Harris, Alfred Edward (1917)
Harrison, William (1916)
Hart, Martin Frank (1918)
Hart, Reginald George (1915)
Harvey, John William (1915)
Haskins, Clifford Herbert
   (1916)
Haskins, Ernest John (1916)
Haslehurst, Ernest Chapman
   (1915)
Hatherway, William Frank
   (1916)
Hawkins, John Stephen
   (1917)
Hawthorne, J. (1917)
Hayman, Hubert Frederick
   (1916)
Hayman, John Winsor (1917)

Haynes, Thomas Norman
(1919)
Hayward, Hubert Sidney
(1915)
Hayward, Wilfred Frederick
Haywood, Edward Charles
(1917)
Hebditch-Carter, Henry
Homer James (1915)
Hedgecock, William Ernest
(1917)
Hedley, John George
Hempson, W.
Henning, Richard James
(1917)
Hewitt, G.
Hibbs, A.J.
Hibbs, E.H.
Hibberd, Arthur Albert
(1916)
Hilliar, Albert (1918)
Hills, D.G.
Hitchcock, Harold (1917)
Hoare, Richard John (1916)
Hockey, Joseph Ernest (1915)
Hockey, Thomas J. (1914)
Hodge, Percy (1914)
Holdway, Charles
Holgate, Sidney
Holland, W.
Holloway, Albert Benjamin
George (1920)
Holloway, J.T.
Holloway, Joseph T.
Holloway, Sidney Albert
(1917)
Homer, G.J.

Honeybun, Philip
Hopkins, Henry Charles
(1914)
Hordle, Alfred Samuel
(1916)
Hordle, Sidney
Hosier, Ernest
Hosking, H.
Houghton, E.W.
Houlton, Arthur James
(1916)
Hounsell, John William
(1915)
Howman, Claude Knox
(1915)
Hudson, Henry William
(1915)
Hughes, Charles Edward
(1916)
Hughes, Joseph (1918)
Hughes, Richard (1916)
Humby, Charles William
(1918)
Hunt, Harry Joe (1919)
Hunt, Ivor Stephen (1915)
Hunt, Percy Edwin (1917)
Hunt, Reginald
Huntington, Harry Thomas
(1918)
Hustler, Harold Tom (1918)
Hustler, R.G. (1917)
Hutchings, George Conrad
Victoria Parrot (1917)
Hutchings, Herbert George
(1916) Huxter, J.
Huxter, John Albert (1915)
Hyde, Leonard Charles (1919)

Hyde, Leonard Charles
  Reginald Ingram, Bertie
  (1917)

Ingram, John Dorrington
Ings, W.
Inman, Edward
Ivamy, William George
  (1917)

James, Harry (1914)
James, Howard Edward
  Harry (1920)
James, Joseph (1915)
James, Sidney
Janes, Alfred William
  (1917)
Jeans, Arthur Alfred (1918)
Jeans, Frederick George
  (1915)
Jeffrey, W.G.
Jenkins, Frank (1916)
Jenkins, Harry Ralph (1917)
Jennings, Neville
Johnson, Al
Johnson, Alfred
Johnson, H.
Johnson, Thomas (1917)
Johnstone, Edmund Leake
  Burns (1918)
Joiner, W.
Jones, Archibald Ellis (1917)
Jones, E.V. (1915)
Jordan, L.W.
Jordan, L.W.
Joyce, A.E.
Joyce, A. (1916)

Joyce, Frederick William
  Tidbury (1919)
Jupp, F.G. (1916)

Kearly, John
Keene, Clarence Frederick
Keene, P.E.
Kendall, William
Kerr, Norman
Kiddle, Everard John
King, James
King, Robert Lambirth
King, Stewart
King, William
Kingsbury, William Charles
  (1914)
Kingsbury, Ernest Samson
  (1917)
Kingsnorth, Frank
Kirkwood, Robert
Kitcatt, Edward (1918)
Kitcher, W.V.
Knight, P.

Lacey, A.J.
Lacey, Frederick George
Lacey, G.F.
Lacey, William Charles Cecil
Lafford, George Vernon
  (1917)
Lake, C.
Lake, E.
Lake, Ernest Harry (1916)
Lake, F.L.
Lake, Fred (1915)
Lake, G.S.
Lake, George Sidney (1918)

Lamb, J.A.

Lander, W.H.H.

Landray, William Henry Hubert (1916)

Lane, H.A.

Langford, A.

Langford, L.

Law, Edward Michael Fitzgerald (1918)

Law, Robert Archibald Fitzgerald (1918)

Lawrence, A.K.

Lawrence, Humphrey Richard Locke (1915)

Lawrence, J.L.

Lax, H.

Le Brun, Lewis Appleby (1918)

Lee, A.H.

Lee, G.A. (1919)

Legg, Frederick Walter (1916)

Legg, Harry (1917)

Legg, T. (1918)

Legg, Victor George Lewis (1919)

Le Lievre, Alfred Henry John (1917)

Lemmon, William (1919)

Lewis

Light, William Edward (1914)

Lilley, Leo (1915)

Lillington, Alfred Ernest

Lillington, Alfred Henry (1917)

Limbrick, J.L. (1916)

Lind, Charles Frederick (1918)

Livermore, William (1917)

Lloyd, Reginald Carey (1917)

Loader, Thomas Frederick (1917)

Loader, W.G. (1917)

Locke, C.

Lockyer, W. (1918)

Lodge, Harold Andrew (1918)

Looker, Nesta Mary (1919)

Lovelace, Reginald Robert (1918)

Loveless, Malcolm Mitchell (1917)

Lovell, Edgar Cecil (1917)

Lovell, William James (1918)

Lugg, Reginald Foster (1916)

Luther, Frederick George (1916)

Luther, William James (1918)

Macdonald, Neville Douglas (1918)

Macey, J.

Mack, J.

Macreight, A.W.J.

Maidment, Andrew (1914)

Maidment, D.C. (1916)

Maidment, W.C. (1917)

Maidment, George William (1916)

Manuel, James Ambrose (1918)

Maple, J.J.

Marchant, A. (1919)

Marsh, E.V.

Marsh, J.

Martin, David (1919)

Martin, H.
Martin, T.H.
Masterman, Frederick (1916)
Masterman, W.G. (1918)
Masters, George William
 (1918)
Masters, Harold Charles
 Brownsea (1916)
Masters, N.C. (1918)
Matthew, W.C.
Matthews, Albert Edward
 (1918)
Mauleverer, Claude (1917)
Maynard, A.
McCreight, Arthur
McGregor, G.B. (1917)
McKay, E.H.
McMullen, Frank (1914)
Meads, Arthur Charles (1914)
Medland, William Harry
 Wilson (1914)
Merrifield, Ernest (1917)
Merrifield, William (1917)
Miller, Alfred (1918)
Miller, Howard
Miller, Frederick James
 Victor (1922)
Miller, Harrie Reginald (1918)
Miller, William Herbert
 Henry (1916)
Milne, William
Mitchell, Arthur M.M. (1918)
Mitchell, Arthur W.
Mitchell, C.E.
Mitchell, Frank Henry (1915)
Mitchell, Herbert Edward
 (1918)

Mockridge, George Ewart
 (1916)
Mollen, I.J.
Monnery, Walter (1917)
Morrell, Bernard Joseph
 (1916)
Morris, Charles George
 (1914)
Morris, Frank Milton (1918)
Mottashaw, George Oliver
 (1918)
Moxham, Reginald (1916)
Mumford, Sydney Francis
 (1918)
Musslewhite, Charles (1914)
Musslewhite, G. (1918)
Munden, Bert (1916)

Neville, Walter John (1917)
Newbury, H.
Newman, A.J.
Nobbs, Harry Ernest (1918)
Nobes, William Frank (1916)
Norman, Charles Thomas
 (1918)
Norman, Ernest Charles
 (1918)
Norman, George Reginald
 (1915)
Notley, Guy (1917)

Oates, Harry George James
 (1916)
Ockford, William Ernest John
 (1918)
Old, A.W. (1917)
Old, S.C. (1918)

Oliver, Frederick James (1918)
Orchard, Stephen Edward
  (1915)
Osborne, H.C. (1917)
Osmond, Albert George
  Taylor (1918)
Osmond, Edgar J.S.
Osmond
Ox, A.J.S. (1916)

Packer, Robert Wallace (1918)
Paice, Nicholas John (1919)
Paine, George Gordon (1918)
Palmer, W.J. (1918)
Park, Arthur John (1917)
Parker, Frederick
Paul, L.E.C.
Pavstorne, Geoffrey
Pearce, Harrie Herbert (1918)
Pearce, H.C.
Penney, Ernest (1915)
Penney, H.
Penney, P.B.B.
Penny, Ernest
Penny, P.B.P. (1918)
Peplow, John (1917)
Percy, F.
Perry, J.F.S.
Perry, W.A.
Peters, W.A.H.
Petersen, Donald
Petersen, Percy (1917)
Phillips, A.C.
Phillips, F.
Phillips, J.R. (1917)
Phillips, W.
Phillpot, W.E. (1916)

Philpotts, William Ernest
  (1916)
Pinn, F.J.G. (1917)
Pittman, Arthur (1918)
Pogue, Reginald T.
Polley, William
Pool, Leonard
Poole, Frederick George
  (1917)
Pond, Albert Reginald (1918)
Pond, E.E.
Ponton, E.A.
Ponton, Ernest
Pontifex, Dudley Allen
Potter, William
Pridham, A.T.
Pridham, F.D.
Pritchard, P.A.
Pritchard, Philip Noel (1918)
Purdy, William Henry (1914)
Pym, Frank (1917)

Rabbetts, William
Randall, William
Rawlins, Hugh
Rayner, A.
Read, A.J.
Read, James
Read, Reverend C.C .R.
Read, Samuel James Stockley
Read, W.
Reader, E.G.
Real, W.B.
Real, William Bond
Redhead, Leonard
Redhead, M.
Redhead, William Maurice

Reeks, G.
Rice, Nathaniel
Richards, H.B.
Richardson, Tom
Richie, H.
Ricketts, Edgar Gerald
Riggs, E.J.
Riggs, F.A.
Riggs, Sidney Albert
Rigler, Charles George
Rigler, Thomas
Robbins, A.G.
Roberts, F.E.
Roberts, Herbert
Roberts, John
Robins, F.
Robinson, D.M.G.
Robinson, L.A.
Roder, John Edward
Rogers, A.S.
Rogers, Frederick James
Rogers, George Albert
Rogers, Leonard
Rogers, William Thomas
   Henry
Ronaldson, John Kirkland
Rose, J.
Rose, Merton A.
Routledge, Thomas
Rudge, Frederick John
Rudge, William Alfred
Rundle, C.N.
Rundle, C.S.
Russell, Robert W.
Ryder, J.
Sampson, Leslie L.
Samways, H.

Sanford, Harry Herbert
Sansom, B.J.
Sargent, H.
Sargent, S.J.
Saunders, Albert
Saunders, Arthur
Saunders, Frederick
   Charles
Saunders, Henry John
Scammell, Lily
Schofield, R.I.
Scott, Arthur
Scott, Charles
Seaman, J.
Sellers, Arthur
Serjent, Frederick John
Sharp, A.A.C.

Sharp, Reginald Auberon
   Herbert
Shave, G.
Shave, Leslie Harry
Shearing, H.
Shergold, William
Sherwood, Bertie
Short, Percy
Short, Sidney Ernest
Shortridge, Frank
Sibley, Lewis
Simmons, W.
Simms, Percy
Sims, Frederick H.
Skinner, Frederick A.
Skinner, H.
Skinner, Jesse
Skinner, Thomas
Skinner, William

Skuce, F.
Smith, A.G.
Smith, Alfred Owen
Smith, C.F.
Smith, G.
Smith, George
Smith, Harold Roland
Smith, J.
Smith, J.
Smith, John
Smith, W.H.
Speck, J.
Spencer-Sprake, John
   Frederick
Squibb, B.R .J.
Squires, George Victor
Stabley, S.
Stainer, Cecil George
Staley, J.A.
Steel, Frank
Stephens, W.G.
Strickland, F.
Stone, Robert Leonard Austin
Stone, William John
Stout, George James
Sturgess, Samuel E.
Sutton, William Thomas
Sweeney, E.
Sweet, Roy Thornhill
Sweetapple, Frederick

Taylor, Albert James
Taylor, Gilbert Frank
Taylor, Thomas
Teague, Frederick George
Thorne, Archibald George
Tilley, Harry Percival

Tollerfield, William Charles
Toop, G.R.
Toop, W.G.
Townsend, J.W.E.
Trent, G.J.
Trickett, William Arthur
Trowbridge, Charles James
Tucker, Percival Andrew
Tucker, W.J.
Turner, A.G.
Turner, H.
Turner, N.
Turner, Robert Nathaniel
Turner, R.T.
Turner, W.T.

Underhay, William Frederick
   George
Upshell, Samuel Christmas
Upward, Frank

Van Goethem, H.E.
Van Schapdael, Francis
   Harold
Vanner, Charles James
Veal, W.H.
Vincent, R.G.
Vine, Frederick
Wadham, Francis William
   Douglas
Ward, Harry
Wareham, William Henry
Warren, Albert Edward
Warren, Edwin Montague
Warry, Charles Victor
Washer, W.C.
Waters, James Herbert

Watmore, Tom Harold
Watson, W.
Watton, F.
Watts, C.W.
Wear, A.L.
Webb, Arthur Leonard
Webb, Edgar H.
Weeks, A.
Weir, James
Wellman, Frederick
Whalley, Kenneth
Wheeler, Frank
Wheeler, H.J.T.
Wheeler, P.
Whiffen, Frank George
Whitaker, Robert Leversley
White, A.
Whittle, Charles Edward
Whittle, E.C.
Whittle, Edward C.
Whittle, John Tilsed
Whittle, R.
Whitty, Cyril
Whitty, Edward C.
Whitty, Percy John
Wilcox, F.
Wilkins, W.

Williams, E.W.
Willis, W.
Wills, Edward Robert
Wills, Frederick George
Wills, John Alfred
Wills, Thomas John
Wilson, Charles
Wilson, George Frank
Wilson, Turle Barber
Witchell, William Arthur
  Elliott
Withnell, W.H.
Wood, William Allen
Woodland, Sidney A.
Woodland, William Henry
Woodman, S.G.
Woolaway, Arthur
Woolfries, Edwin
Woolfries, James
Wyldbere-Smith, H.F.

Yeates, A.
Yeoman, Reginald George
Young, C.F.
Young, H.G.
Young, Harry
Young, J.S.

It is hoped that everybody who was born in Poole, lived there or otherwise had a connection with the town has been included, and that there are no misspelled surnames, Christian names or errors with initials. The author apologizes for any unintended oversights.

As with such matters, there is always some debate, even disagreement, as to who should or should not be included on such a list, and exactly which area is covered by these same individuals.

Most name omissions from war memorials or rolls of honour have occurred accidently. If a family moved away from their village or town during the course of the war, it might not have been known whether a son, brother or father who served in the war had survived or been killed. There would have been people who were born in Poole but moved away before they enlisted for wartime service. Some towns and villages refused to include the names of men on their war memorials when it was learned that they had been shot at dawn for 'cowardice'. Sometimes a name was misspelled or wrong initials included. There were cases of men serving under assumed names, and when they were killed, it was easy for them to slip through the 'net' and not be included on any town or village's memorial.

Here is an example of such complications. Private 10711 George Angell, who served with the 5th Battalion, Dorsetshire Regiment, sadly died of his wounds on 27 September 1916. That information, including the spelling of his surname, is taken from the British army's medal rolls index cards, which record the wartime service medals to which each man was entitled.

The 1911 handwritten census shows a George Angel working on a farm with his father Fred and his brother John. He lived with his parents, Fred and Bessie Angel, at Affpuddle in Dorset, along with brothers John Reginald, Percy Harry, Walter, Robert and his sisters Amelia, Alice and Emily. The roll of honour for those men from Poole who died as a result of having served their country and includes those who lost their lives in the course of the Great War can be found on the website www.pooleatwar. co.uk. This includes George Angel, who it shows as having served in 'A' Company, 5th Battalion, Dorsetshire Regiment and as someone who lived in Poole. He died on 27 September 1916 at the age of 26 while serving in France. He was buried at the Contay British Cemetery in the Somme region. On another roll of honour compiled by Poole History Centre, which lists the names of the men from Poole who lost their lives during the Great War, the name George Angel is not included.

A check of the Commonwealth War Graves website shows two men with the name of George Angel: one of them, George

Theodore Angel, was a private in the Welsh Fusiliers; and the other, George Frederick Angel, was a private in the Royal Marine Light Infantry. Neither man had any connection with Poole and there was no trace of a George Angel of the 5th Battalion, Dorsetshire Regiment. However, checking the same website and searching for George Angell shows he was there. It shows that his parents were Fred and Bessie Angell living at Hill Butts, Wimbourne, in Dorset, not Poole.

The author then searched the British army's service records for soldiers who served in the Great War and found one in the name of George Angell that actually had a signature on it with the surname clearly spelled Angell. He was 21 years of age, lived at Marnhull Pit, Hill Butts, Wimborne, Dorset and had enlisted in the town on 7 September 1914, becoming a Private (10711) in the 5th (Service) Battalion, Dorsetshire Regiment, confirming that this was the man in question.

So despite George Angel having purportedly lived in Poole, no direct evidence of it could be found. There were only references to him having lived in Wimborne, with the spelling of his surname as Angell. It did, however, show not only how difficult it can be researching individuals from the Great War period but how easy it would have been for discrepancies to arise resulting in somebody being incorrectly omitted from, or added to, a war memorial or a roll of honour.

It should be added that despite the issue around whether George Angell should or shouldn't have been included on a Poole roll of honour commemorating those who lost their lives during the Great War, George's brothers John and Percy were also killed.

John, who enlisted in the army on the same day and at the same location as George, had the service number 10712. He was killed in action at Gallipoli on 7 August 1915. Percy, who was known by his middle name of Harry, served with the 6th Battalion, Dorsetshire Regiment and was killed in action on the Western Front in France on 23 August 1918.

CHAPTER EIGHT

Holton Heath Cordite Factory

During the Great War the need arose to build a cordite factory for the Royal Navy. The chosen location was Holton Heath, an area of Wareham St Martin, Dorset, situated 6 miles to the west of Poole. Today, taking the A350 and A35 roads, it is a journey driveable in about fifteen minutes.

The building of the factory came about at the insistence of the then First Lord of the Admiralty, Winston Churchill, who believed that it wasn't just important but essential for the Royal Navy to have their own supply of cordite. Holton Heath was chosen as the site for several reasons. It was a remote setting, well

Holton Heath Cordite Factory.

away from any heavily-populated areas, and it was close to both sea and train transport links. Poole Harbour was close by, as was the London and South Western Railway line, which ran from London to Plymouth via Salisbury and Exeter. The location also provided the use of the A351 Wareham to Poole main road.

To enable uninterrupted transportation of the finished cordite from the factory, a railway station was opened at Holton Heath, linked to the main railway line by a siding. The station and the railway line running through it were purely for the transportation of cordite and not used for public purposes until 1924.

The manufacture of cordite required a constant supply of water. This was achieved by building a coal-fired water pumping house for the purpose of making water directly available to the factory; this was taken from the nearby River Stour.

Once manufactured, the cordite would be transported to Poole Harbour and from a specially-constructed jetty it would then be taken by boat to the Royal Navy's armaments depot at Priddy's Hard in nearby Gosport.

Mention is made of this munitions factory because many of the women who worked there were from Poole. It was a relatively attractive proposition to become what had affectionately become known as a 'munitionette' as not only were such girls well paid, earning 20s a week, but their train fares from Poole were also paid. Such was the desire to have young women from the Poole area to work at Holton Heath that Captain Desborough, responsible for acquiring women to work at the factory, invited the mayor and other members of the local Corporation to view the facilities so they could see for themselves the working conditions of the town's young women. There was even a hostel at the factory if the girls preferred to stay there rather than enduring the daily commute to and from Poole.

The production and manufacture of cordite required large amounts of the solvent acetone, otherwise known as propanone. It is a colourless liquid, both volatile and flammable, and mainly because of the war it was in short supply. Before 1912 the process of making acetone involved the distillation of wood, but then a biochemist named Chaim Weizmann developed a process for producing acetone through bacterial fermentation, vitally important to the British war effort. In 1917 there was a grain shortage, so horse chestnuts (conkers), a source of starch, were used instead, with a number of large silos being built for storage. Yet despite adults and children countrywide being asked to collect horse chestnuts by the Ministry of Munitions, they were only used in the making of acetone for three months as they proved to be a poor source of starch.

An explosion occurred at Holton Heath Cordite Factory just before 1.00 am on Saturday, 15 November 1919. The initial report was followed by others and the subsequent flames were visible for miles around. One person – 32-year-old Jesse Orchard who lived at 'Glencoe', Lester Road, Poole – was killed in the explosion and several others injured.

The explosion in the factory's No. 1 acetone recovery stove, cordite section, killed Jesse instantly. The cordite from which the acetone was being recovered burst into flames, quickly engulfing the premises, and the building was wrecked. Despite extreme danger to themselves, the factory's fire brigade worked bravely and succeeded in preventing the fire from spreading to other areas. If they hadn't, the loss of life could have been much greater. It took them about two hours to bring the fire under control.

An inquest into the accident was opened on the afternoon of Monday, 17 November 1919 at the factory by the deputy coroner for East Dorset, Mr R.D. Maddock. After three witnesses had been called, proceedings were adjourned until the following day so that His Majesty's Inspector of Factories could attend.

Jesse's older brother George, a motor-cycle engineer who lived at 'Tower View', Belmont Road, Upper Parkstone confirmed identification of the deceased and that he had never made any comment to him about potential dangers at the factory.

Clarence Henry Leaper, who lived at 'Rockerville', Wimborne Road, Poole, was a foreman at the factory who had known Jesse since he began working there in 1915. He informed the inquest that he and Jesse had been speaking in his office about the making up of time cards just after midnight on the Saturday. It was a brief conversation after which they went their separate ways, but at about 12.40 am he heard what he described as a 'sharp report' followed by a flash, and then another 'report' noticeably louder than the first. He and his assistant foreman immediately went to see what had happened and at once saw the No. 1 acetone recovery stove was on fire. He had the hose connected up to the hydrants, and aimed them at the adjacent buildings in an effort to prevent them becoming engulfed in flames. A short while later there was another explosion from the area of the No. 1 stove.

Captain Desborough explained the design of the factory's stoves, and how the cordite was placed in them and dried by means of hot water pipes. He also gave evidence that the fire was eventually extinguished at about 2.30 am after water had been sprayed on the buildings and surrounding grassy areas. Jesse Orchard had still not been located and hadn't been seen since before the first explosion. A search was then made among the debris and Orchard's body was discovered at the rear of the No. 1 stove. The walls were blown down and the masonry of the No. 1 section was completely wrecked.

Dr Frank O. Bell from Wareham said that on being informed of the accident, he travelled with Inspector W. Deacon to the factory. On arrival, he was informed that a body had been found under a large mass of fallen concrete, the result of the explosion. Dr Bell determined that the man's death would have been instantaneous, and caused by shock consistent with the brickwork having fallen on him.

After the three witnesses gave their evidence, the inquest was adjourned until the following day, allowing His Majesty's Inspector of Factories for Southampton and the surrounding areas, Mr A.F.J. Donnelly, to be in attendance. Also present were Police Superintendent H. Toop from Wareham, Mr J. Emery from the Workers' Union, Major Wellsford from the Admiralty, Mr William T. Thompson, the manager of the factory, and the Superintendent of Works Captain Desborough.

Mr Thompson, who lived at St Peter's Road, Parkstone, told the inquest that he had been in charge of the Holton Heath factory since it opened. He then outlined Jesse Orchard's role and that it involved taking and controlling the temperatures. In the course of his ordinary duties, he also took the temperature of the stove's door before going to the rear of the stove to regulate its overall temperature by opening or closing the vapour valve, although Mr Thompson emphasized there was absolutely no chance of an explosion taking place during this procedure. At the time of the explosion there was a north-north-east wind blowing, ranging from 16 to 18 mph, and the temperature between 9.00 pm and 3.00 am was around 32 degrees, freezing point. In his opinion the explosion had occurred due to the nitroglycerine having evaporated from the drying cordite, resulting in vapour forming in the valve due to the cold. When in a half-frozen condition it was more sensitive and more likely to explode than otherwise, but proper outlets to remove the accumulations of nitroglycerine were fitted to the valve as a safeguard. The valve was made of zinc. If the nitroglycerine was frozen, the act of opening and closing the valve would probably cause friction; this might result in its detonation and the flame would in turn backfire and ignite the vapour and the stove. This was, in Mr Thompson's opinion, the cause of the explosion. In case of freezing, the usual method adopted was to apply hot-water cloths to the pipes in order to thaw the nitroglycerine and this process removed the danger.

Mr Thompson continued that one of the rules of the factory was that in the case of defective machinery, the chemist in charge should be immediately informed. Nitroglycerine in the pipes, even during summertime, would become increasingly sensitive as a result of extremes of either heat or cold. The valves might be enclosed, but it was not certain if this would increase or decrease the risk of using the valve.

Mr Thompson next produced a photograph of the scene of the accident soon after it had taken place. From what he knew of Jesse Orchard, he was a careful and methodical worker who would not have used undue pressure in opening or closing the valve. If the accident had been caused in that way, it would have been through an error of judgement. It was possible that if nitroglycerine was frozen in the valve, there might have been liquid nitroglycerine obtained from the pipe, leading Jesse to have incorrectly believed it was clear when it was not.

The coroner said there was a melancholy satisfaction in that Mr Orchard's death must have been instantaneous, it was probably due to shock caused by the explosion and there was no suggestion of negligence on anyone's part. He also emphasized that the greatest care in the avoidance of accidents had always been taken at the factory, as borne out by its safety record. He added that he believed it was the only factory of its kind in the United Kingdom that had not had an injurious accident during the entire war. The jury returned a verdict that Mr Orchard had died of shock caused by being crushed by falling masonry as a direct result of the explosion.

Captain Desborough said that on behalf of himself and everyone at the factory, he wished to express his deepest sympathy to the relatives of Mr Orchard who, he added, 'had been a most excellent worker.' The coroner and the jury also expressed their sympathy. Mr Orchard's funeral took place on the afternoon of Wednesday, 19 November 1919 at Longfleet cemetery after a service at the North Street Primitive Methodist Church by the Reverend J. Lambert Baggott. Besides his widow and other close family members, there was a large turnout of staff from the factory, management and workers alike. There were also members of the Workers' Union, from both the local and national bodies.

At the time of the 1911 census Jesse was aged 24, working as a plastic mould-maker and living at 17 Glencoe Road, Upper Parkstone with his parents Seth and Fanny, his brother Bertie who worked as a clock repairer, and his sister Ada. There were three other brothers – George, Harry and William – and a sister Blanche, who had all left home by 1911.

Jesse married Evelyn Marlow in August 1914 at Poole, and they set up home at Lester Road in the town. At the time of his death, Jesse left Evelyn £354 2s 5d in his will (about £19,000 in 2018); a substantial sum of money.

Sources

1911 Census of England
Army Registers of Soldiers' Effects, 1901–1929
Dorset Electoral Register, 1839–1922
Nursing Registers, UK & Ireland (1898–1968)
Royal Navy Registers of Seamen's Services, 1848–1939
Royal Navy and Royal Marine War Graves Roll, 1914–1919
Bournemouth Guardian
Indian *Sunday Times*
www.cwgc.com
www.ancestry.co.uk
www.britishnewspaperarchive.co.uk
Wikipedia
www.eztis.myzen.co.uk
www.pooleww1.org.uk

Index

About the Author

Stephen is a happily retired police officer, having served with Essex Police as a constable for thirty years between 1983 and 2013. He is married to Tanya who is also his best friend.

Both his sons, Luke and Ross, were members of the armed forces, collectively serving five tours of Afghanistan between 2008 and 2013. Both were injured on their first tour. This led to Stephen's first book, *Two Sons in a Warzone – Afghanistan: The True Story of a Father's Conflict*, published in October 2010.

Both his grandfathers served in and survived the Great War, one with the Royal Irish Rifles, the other in the Merchant Navy, while his father was a member of the Royal Army Ordnance Corp (ROAC) during the Second World War.

Stephen corroborated with one of his writing partners, Ken Porter, on a book published in August 2012, *German POW Camp 266 – Langdon Hills*, which spent six weeks as the number one best-selling book in Waterstones, Basildon between March and April 2013. Steve and Ken collaborated on a further four books in the 'Towns & Cities in the Great War' series by Pen & Sword. Stephen has also written other titles in the same series of books, and in February 2017 his book *The Surrender of Singapore: Three Years of Hell 1942–45* was published. This was followed in March 2018 by *Against All Odds: Walter Tull, the Black Lieutenant*.

Stephen has also co-written three crime thrillers which were published between 2010 and 2012 and centre around a fictional detective named Terry Danvers.

When he is not writing, Stephen and Tanya enjoy the simplicity of walking their three German Shepherd dogs early each morning, at a time when most sensible people are still fast asleep in their beds.